THE NOBLE ROOM

THE NOBLE ROOM

*The Inspired Conception and Tumultuous Creation
of Frank Lloyd Wright's Unity Temple*

David M. Sokol

FOREWORD BY Sidney K. Robinson

THE WORSHIP OF GOD
THE SERVICE OF MAN

TOP FIVE BOOKS

A TOP FIVE BOOK

Published by Top Five Books, LLC

521 Home Avenue, Oak Park, Illinois 60304

www.top-five-books.com

Library of Congress Catalog Number: 2008906617

ISBN: 978-0-9789270-3-5

Book and cover design by Top Five Books.
Front cover skylight photography by and courtesy of Jan Theun van Rees
Back cover and endsheet photography © 2008 Lisa Kelly, Prairie Design Group

*All photos and illustrations courtesy The Frank Lloyd Wright Foundation
unless otherwise indicated.*

*This project was supported by a grant from the
Graham Foundation for Advanced Studies in the Fine Arts.*

100th ANNIVERSARY EDITION
Printed and bound in Canada
10 9 8 7 6 5 4 3 2 1

To the past and present members of both
Unity Temple Restoration Foundation and the
Unity Temple Unitarian Universalist Congregation in Oak Park,
for their patience and support in seeing this
volume through its long gestation.

Also by David M. Sokol:

John Quidor: Painter of American Legend, 1973

American Architecture & Art: A Guide to Information Sources, 1976

*American Art: Painting, Sculpture, Architecture, Decorative
    Arts, Photography* (coauthor), 1979

*American Decorative Arts and Old World Influences: A Guide
    to Information Sources*, 1980

Life in Nineteenth-Century America, 1981

Solitude: Inner Visions in American Art, 1982

*Two Hundred Years of American Painting for Private
    Chicago Collections*, 1983

American Art: American Vision, Paintings from a Century of Collecting
    (coauthor), 1990

*A Guide to Oak Park's Frank Lloyd Wright and Prairie School
    Historic District* (coauthor), 1999

Oak Park, Illinois: Continuity and Change, 2000

*Engaging with the Present: The Contribution of the American Jewish
    Artists Club to Modern Art in Chicago, 1928–2004*, 2004

Otto Neumann: His Life and Work, 2007

CONTENTS

ILLUSTRATIONS

Chapter 4

Chapter 5

Chapter 6

Chapter 7

ARCHITECTURAL EVOLUTION OF UNITY TEMPLE

Unity Temple is a particularly eloquent demonstration of Wright's architectural goals because we can uncover the steps that he took to design it. His subsequent explanations of the development of the design for Unity Temple in *An Autobiography* (1932, 1943) provide further indications of what he was trying to achieve in this building. His detailed narrative of the design process, written some twenty-five years after the fact, and his amendments to that narrative clearly indicate Unity Temple's importance to the unfolding of his architectural career. Wright actually "constructed" Unity Temple several times: three major stages of design, adjustments during construction, and twice in words as he changed the description of it from the first to the second editions of his *Autobiography*. This foreword will explore how and why both the design and the explanation changed.

As this book effectively demonstrates, the building on the corner of Lake Street and Kenilworth in Oak Park, Illinois, can be approached from several directions. The place that Unity Temple holds in Wright's architectural career is significant as judged by Wright himself and by others concerned with a new "style" of modern architecture or as an important example of Wright's "organic architecture."

Figure 1. The exterior of Unity Temple (left) is based on an architectural tradition of solid, axial symmetry. A new architecture is evident in the interior (right), whose oak strips over painted plaster create a continuous enclosure of light, folded planes. Photos courtesy Sidney K. Robinson

Previous considerations of Unity Temple from these various perspectives have uncovered significant material that precedes and informs the observations made here (see the bibliography).

Standing on Lake Street in Oak Park, one is confronted by an edifice that is, at the same time, an immovable object and a transitional stage in the evolution of Wright's architecture. For an architect who is known for insisting on the "continuity" of inside and out, Unity Temple presents a surprising contradiction. The rough, massive, opaque exterior in no way prepares one for the light, smooth, thin membrane of the interior (fig. 1). This wide disparity must signal that a point is being made, particularly when one realizes that the design actually began as a display of that very interior/exterior continuity and successively diverged from it.

The first design for the Temple drawn in the autumn of 1905 is much closer to that expectation of continuity between inside and out than is the finished building. The initial proposal, the subject of the memorable perspective by Wright's talented draftsperson, Marion Mahony, was a brick building closely related to Wright's most recent major public building: the Larkin office building in Buffalo, New York (fig. 2). The Larkin Building's assemblage of abstract "blocks" with crisp brick corners is articulated by recesses between the masonry masses and by the stone coping at their tops and bases. The formal set Wright proposed for Unity Temple is a direct outgrowth of this recently finished commercial building.

The Larkin Building had attracted notice for its starkness and was considerably larger than Unity Temple, but Wright chose Unity Temple, not Larkin, to explain his design process in his *Autobiography*. Contrary to the solid, cliff-like, appearance of the Larkin Building, its blocky volumes were not bearing masonry, but brick

Figure 2. The immediate predecessor of Unity Temple is the steel-frame, brick-veneer Larkin Building in Buffalo, New York.

surfaces supported by a steel frame. Wright, of course, was familiar with the steel frame from the buildings going up in Chicago when he arrived there in 1887 and from the major buildings he worked on while he was with the architecture firm of Adler and Sullivan. And yet he built significantly with the steel frame only this once in his career. So what was the problem? Why did he avoid using it and, when he did use it, why did he avoid talking about it? It is important to note that Wright had just used concrete in the repetitive structure appropriate for the 1905 factory for the E-Z Polish company.

Separating the steel structure that holds up a building from the brick walls that enclose it meant that Larkin was only a partial success in Wright's architectural evolution. His goal, which may be what his infamous word *organic* is all about, was an integral building, singular and unified, where enclosure and structure are not separate, but continuous. Unity Temple began as a brick enclosure of a concrete structure, a separation not unlike the Larkin Building. When it became a completely concrete building, even if the motivation was inevitably economic, Wright began to explore continuity in terms beyond the fairly obvious one of inside and outside.

First Design

The initial proposal for Unity Temple in the fall of 1905 is traditional in some ways and a departure from tradition in others. Its forward-looking design extends and surpasses past models and makes it a singularly revealing demonstration of Wright's architecture. The convention for Unitarian congregational places, as represented by the white, wooden edifice whose conflagration initiated the need for a new facility, was a center-aisle, pitched-roofed, steepled New England church. Whether that was appropriate for the evolving congregation in Oak Park was a question that Wright's design helped to clarify. The flat-roofed, cubic forms of the new Unity Temple were explicitly set against the traditional forms of Western architectural history, if not in the drawings for Unity Temple, then in the perspective of a strikingly similar building Wright designed concurrently with the Oak Park Temple. The Yahara Boat House (fig. 3) in Madison, Wisconsin, definitively redated as being from the same year as Unity Temple, was depicted in a perspective that showed a pointed steeple and a dome (the soon to be completed Wisconsin State Capitol?) in the hills behind the floating slab of the wooden building. This contrast is a rhetorical gesture that sought to displace traditional architectural forms with the new, aggressive, orthogonal slabs, screens, and blocks of Wright's architecture.

The dialogue between convention and Wright's efforts to depart from it makes Unity Temple such an important building. Wright was thirty-six years old; he had been practicing independently for a dozen years. He had had notable successes with stunning residences managing to make, as Robert Twombly so aptly pointed out, the avant-garde "accessible" (1979, 58). The sequence of Unity Temple's design is a revealing record of how Wright struggled to grow new things out of moldering traditions. How very "organic" to grow into something new, rather than to aggressively eliminate the past in a paroxysm of Modernist revolution. This delicate balance between the old and the new ran the risk of being mistaken as an apology for the

Figure 3. Yahara Boat House, Madison, Wisconsin

past, which may account for Wright's often extreme rejection of the very past that he was so creatively digesting.

The first design in brick extends an architectural tradition of axes, dominant centers, a hierarchy of articulated major and minor volumes. They are present in an abstract way, with only minor elaboration of ornament. Its continuity of materials and forms inside and out is a departure from this tradition in some ways because the means of construction are evident both inside and out.

The brick version constructs the crisp, cubic masses that Wright later referred to as "screens" (but more of that later) using the convention of masonry walls with bases and caps of concrete playing the same role as the red sandstone in the Larkin Building.

The interior of the brick version of Unity Temple also exhibits the forms of construction one would reasonably project from the exterior. Like the Larkin Building, the design of Unity Temple begins by bringing the brick masonry inside with the four piers that differentiate the basically square space into a traditional Greek cross plan. The mixture of masonry and plaster on the inside is exactly what is found in both the Larkin Building and the large prairie style house Wright built for the owner of the Larkin company, Darwin Martin.

The bilateral symmetry of Unity Temple is more stable and centered than the rectangular Larkin Building. The centralized space establishes a vertical axis that creates an integral, organic singularity more effectively than the Larkin Building.

The interior of the brick version of Unity Temple exhibits several examples of traditional construction. The large, brick piers, so clearly supporting the flat roof, are the most prominent structural feature. The point where the piers connect to the roof slab they are supporting is called the "capital." Articulating the top of a column or pier is an age-old practice, both for structural efficiency and expressive clarity. The capital draws attention to that point where structural loads are transferred from horizontal to vertical. Post and beam construction is as traditional as it gets. The tops of Unity Temple's brick piers are articulated at just that

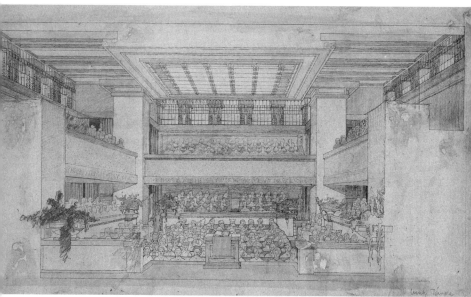

Figure 4. The initial presentation drawing shows an interior that continues the brick-and-concrete construction of the exterior.

Figure 5. The critical structural point—where the weight of the roof is transferred to the square, brick piers—is an ambiguous transition that begins the substitution of continuous, flowing surfaces for clear, structural parts.

place, but the abacus, a part of the capital, the structural block that is the transition between the vertical and horizontal structural elements, is actually represented as a negative space instead of a solid block. This primary tectonic moment, even in this initial version, is being interpreted in a peculiar way: structural transfer is occurring in a void, marked by wooden frame outlining the absent structural element.

The ceiling supported by these piers is divided by wooden members that are not quite structural, but are of a size and in locations that suggest paired roof joists bearing on the columns just outside the clerestory windows. The balcony fronts that span between the corner piers are "carried" above large wooden members that, although not structurally sufficient to do the job, are also of a size and position that correlates with a conventional structural function.

The interior of the first design begins as a traditional tectonic expression of its apparent construction. Of course, architectural articulations that show construction are sometimes merely representations, but the intent is clear that the initial project for Unity Temple is based on a more familiar tradition of indicating how the building is built.

Wright's transformation of tradition is evident even in the development of a specific detail. The ornament on the short columns outside the clerestory windows began, in the initial brick version, as naturalistic branches: curved and with identifiable leaves. As the redesign of the interior proceeded, the branches straightened out, the leaves became geometric, and finally, the vegetal origin nearly disappears, first in square "leaves," and finally by rectangles that are absorbed into the dominant geometric pattern governing the whole building. The interior perspectives reveal the disparity by showing these leaves on the exterior columns through the adjacent geometric pattern of the leaded glass. Wright incrementally abstracts tradition into a new integral continuity from ornament to structure. The leading of the windows themselves is part of this reinterpretation, in this case of Wright's own past, by virtue of their pattern being taken from the Larkin Building's iron fence turned upside down.

The very complete exterior and interior perspectives of the initial design, surely indicating the importance of this hometown commission, are only the beginning of the sequence exploring the relation between the old and the new. Although the placement of the auditorium and the social hall on the lot and their general internal arrangement remain virtually unchanged, considerable effort continued to be expended on designing the interior of the building. It is no wonder that Wright emphasizes the interior space in his subsequent notes and comments, but it is significant that he avoids recounting the struggle to actually design it! This amazing search for a new way of seeing the interior establishes Unity Temple as an important stage of evolution in Wright's career.

The first plans for the building Wright made in the fall of 1905 showed paired aisles entered directly from the narthex entrance link between the auditorium and the secular, gathering space. Changing the entrance sequence from a processional, horizontal axis to a perimeter access reinforces the vertical axis established by the central square plan of the main room. Wright solves the problem of entering a centralized space by raising the floor of the auditorium some four feet, and providing four short stairs along the sides to allow one to slip into the room parallel to the sides. The approach to the auditorium, which has been charted as having at least seven changes in direction, solves the entrance problem by approximating a spiraling into the centralized auditorium space.

Wright makes much of the two "hidden" exits opening directly from the auditorium into the narthex because they allow the departing congregation not to turn their back on the speaker at the lectern. One can take him at his word and believe that the arrangement of exiting from the room is a direct response to functional need, or one can take the position that it was initially a formal arrangement which Wright was creative enough to find use for. Of course, his restatement of Louis Sullivan's dictum "Form Follows Function," to "Form and Function Are One" perfectly demonstrates the interaction between the two, and the mistake of establishing which comes first. This point can also be made with respect to the stimulus for the design as a whole. It may very well be that Wright's architectural goals preexisted the commission by

Figure 6 (left). The tops of the piers in Unity Temple clearly show how structural necessity is absorbed by the oak strips bending over corners of the structure to continue the pattern of the ceiling. Photo courtesy Sidney K. Robinson

Figure 7. An intermediate stage of the interior shown is one of the 1906 perspective drawings that recalls the tops of the piers in the Larkin Building, 1904.

the Unitarian Universalist congregation and were easily accommodated to theological purposes. The alacrity with which Wright uncovered such parallels between form and function, going both ways, served him well throughout his career.

Second Design

The interior as it now exists (fig. 6) appears in one of two perspectives from 1906. Compared to the earlier drawing from 1906 (fig. 7), the large piers, which are no longer drawn as brick, have acquired significant ornamental articulation of their tops, the capital region of these supporting elements. This ornament is directly traceable to the top of the Larkin Building's six-story brick piers. The abacus at the juncture of the piers with the ceiling is no longer a void, but has become a substantial block whose faces have been outlined by a rectangle of wood stripping. There remains a slight recess as the piers penetrate this horizontal block, but the tectonic function is stronger than in the initial brick proposal.

The ceiling in these perspectives is now a grid of squares rather than the leaded glass surface with an axial pattern directed at the lectern. Thin wood strips reaching out to the short columns outside the leaded glass replace heftier wood members. These columns themselves are no longer ornamented by branch and leaf, but more geometric in form, as are their bases, which began as curved cavetto profiles aiding in water shedding only to be changed to rectangular moldings very much like legs on Wright's furniture of the time.

These perspectives now show the interior as an assemblage of smaller piers beside the lectern, and as supports for the balcony fronts each outlined as panels by strips of wood that reinforce their function as separate blocks, supporting or spanning. There are the slightest hints of the bending around corners on these secondary elements, but the dominant reading is one of an assemblage of separate, constructional parts. An important detail is the appearance of light fixtures on the faces of the upper balconies. An ornamental panel to which a pair of globes was attached will remain even after the globes are hung from the ceiling—yet another instance of traces of the past left in the present. Moving the globe lighting from the balcony fronts not only removed an interruption of the planar continuity of the plaster surfaces, it created an ornamental counterpoint to the thin lines and spheres of the lighting fixtures.

Wright's later inscriptions scrawled on these 1906 perspectives indicate what he was discovering here. The annotations on the less finished of the two drawings refers to the Johnson Wax building in Racine (1936) and the effect of the "unlimited overhead," and "space enclosed by screens" (Drexler 1962, pl. 33). On the second perspective, they refer to the "Sense of Space" and "the outside coming in" (Pfeiffer 1985, 57). The direction of this continuity is the reverse of his explanation given in the *Autobiography* where he says: "Let the room inside be the architecture outside" (Wright 1943, 154). The disparity between inside and out noted at the beginning of this chapter either means Wright is inconsistent, or that the continuity flows in both directions.

Working Drawings

The working drawings of 1906 show a third stage in the development of the interior of Unity Temple. These drawings' primary function was to be used by contractors. Large-scale quantities and dimensions are the point, not the ornamental details. But one adjustment to the plans reveals a struggle Wright was facing. The initial design required a tight fit of the stairs in the corners of the auditorium. These stair blocks, so reminiscent of the Larkin Building whose corners themselves underwent substantial adjustments (see Jack Quinan's book: *Frank Lloyd Wright's Larkin Building*, 1989, 2006), are the exterior correlatives of the four interior piers because they articulate the cubic block into the Greek cross. The "arms" of the cross initially projected a foot and a half beyond the corner stair blocks. Had they not done so, the corner volumes would have merged into a singular block. But as the heights of the floors were finalized, and the number of stairs increased from the first to the second level, Wright clarified the "function" of these corner blocks by trying to fit the stairs into the available length of the sides of the corner blocks. To do so he had to make the corner blocks larger, which moved their exterior walls closer to alignment with the terminations of the arms of the Greek cross plan. The separation of the main body of the building from the subsidiary corner blocks was being compromised, but there really was no alternative. The evidence of the compromise is to be found in the first step that overlaps the slit of glass separating the corner block from the main room. This "intrusion" of functional necessity into formal purity is a poignant moment where one can see the consequences of conflicts between two architectural goals, conflicts that even Wright struggled to overcome.

Surprisingly enough, what function those corner blocks were supposed to perform was not clear in the early stages of the design. Their formal importance preceded their functional determination. They contained closets and organ equipment before they were uniquely assigned the function of containing stairs. This uncertainty is curious, considering that their correlatives in the Larkin Building already showed they were stair towers. Their importance as formal elements is further proved by their appearance in the Unity House, where their function is to contain closets.

The interior of the auditorium in the 1906 working drawings is shown in two different versions from one section/elevation to another. Sheet 7 in the set of working drawings shows the piers summarily ornamented by panels outlined by wood stripping. They are clearly not meant to be a "design," but merely a place-holding indication of what would be developed later. Sheet 8 of the working drawings shows the Larkin-derived capitals on the piers. Even at this stage, Wright had not settled on how this new interior would be achieved.

Wright's insistence that the forms of Unity Temple were the result of the material (i.e., concrete) can be misunderstood quite easily. If by "form" one means the overall volumetric articulation of the building, that clearly is not true because these forms are almost exactly the same as in the initial brick version. The impact of cost obviously dictated the rejection of the brick. Now there would be a single material for both structure and enclosure. It is likely that this material continuity stimulated Wright's thinking about continuity in ways that culminated in the design of the revolutionary interior. What is not generally appreciated is how the articulation of base, wall, and cornice in the Larkin Building and in the brick version of Unity Temple was judged so important that Wright went to great lengths to preserve those traditional, tectonic forms in a material that did not require them.

After the decision was made to make Unity Temple all concrete, not brick, Wright proposed that crushed red granite be used as aggregate in the wall portions of the exterior. When that too proved too expensive, he proposed parging the forms with a layer of this colored aggregate concrete and filling the remainder with standard aggregate concrete. Such a complicated process of placement makes little sense and would seem to be proposed only as an extreme effort to preserve the tradition of articulating wall construction by making the walls a different color than base and cornice. Seeing Wright struggle to free himself from the constructional assumptions of traditional architecture is fascinating.

When the material was made continuous concrete, the parts of that traditional construction remained, but the color difference between brick wall and concrete base and coping was eliminated. The exterior of Unity Temple maintains the three-dimensional articulation of the elements of construction even if different materials no longer produce it. The potential of continuous material is only capitalized on in the evolution of the interior, the part of Unity Temple to which Wright drew particular, but only selective, attention.

Wright's later annotations to the second set of interior perspective studies from 1906 are so striking because they avoid these issues when telling the story of designing Unity Temple in his *Autobiography*. The notes on the perspectives are impossible to date with certainty, but may be the result of a retrospective look at his career during H.R. Hitchcock's research for his 1941 book, *In the Nature of Materials*. Wright's own autobiographical narrative can be cited as evidence of his prevarication, his remaking history to satisfy his constantly changing need to be seen in flattering lights. I propose, however, to see it as further "construction," providing insight into his evolution as an architect rather than simply as evidence of a flawed human being.

Unity Temple in the *Autobiography*

The most extensive commentary Wright made on Unity Temple's significance lies in the eight pages in the *Autobiography* where he proposes to describe the design process twenty-five years after the fact. The 1932 version was revised in 1943. How they differ, what is added, what is taken out, and what remains the same give us further clues why Unity Temple was so important to Wright.

When Wright sat down in the late 1920s with his new wife and put together articles for *Liberty* magazine, he reflected on the sixty years of his life and searched for a structure of inevitability for his career and his architecture. These thoughts provided the setting for his reconsideration of Unity Temple. What he felt he had done was to uncover, by peeling back the layers of accumulated convention, the original condition of architecture. As he wrote, he constructed Unity Temple as an inevitable creation. Ancestors, lineage, principle all were called upon to lead back to authentic beginnings. Right from the opening of his description of Unity Temple, he sets up the opposition between it and churches that were built from accumulated tradition where "sentimentality was sense" (Wright 1943, 153). This false way of creating an image, a façade, was the result of misguided intentions.

The desire to present the design as inevitable, as unarguable, led Wright to claim that the design rose out of a deductive process where parts were the necessary consequences of the whole. "Inner spirit" would work itself out from generals to particulars. This is the desired process of design and the desired lesson to be learned from inspecting Unity Temple. But the struggle with the design of the interior belies this ideal certainty. Even Wright's narrative is structured to establish an uninterrupted momentum from client meeting to supper, to nighttime work in the studio, to morning, to several days of working out the "subordinate mass," i.e., Unity House. Revealing the actual search would seem to make the process too vulnerable. To have done so may have helped other people to learn how the struggle to design actually connected to human activities generally, but it put at risk the identification of the architect working like a force of nature: inexorably driven to perfect conclusions.

The process that led inevitably to Unity Temple began with "the philosophy": mind preceded matter; mind acting according to its own nature, unconditioned by habits and influences; mind pure and direct. In the first edition of *An Autobiography*, Wright identified the human activity that had distracted architecture and art. Literature was the enemy. Writing was what confused a vigorous mind creating form. The literary, verbal symbol diverted attention away from the immediate apprehension of mind through material form.

An early instance of Wright revising the way he explains Unity Temple in the *Autobiography* are the three sentences on the evils of literature that he took out in the second edition. Why he did so may say something about his realization that this version of Unity Temple was, itself, literature. These sentences chastising literature pulled the plug on his own verbal construction. The word, whose power he had uncomfortably acknowledged in response to reading Victor Hugo's *Notre Dame de Paris*'s chapters on the history of architecture, the word he had called the "all devouring monster of the age" (1953, bk.3, pt.2, 65) in his remembrances of Louis Sullivan in his 1925 tribute, would not disappear behind the architecture.

The first move Wright describes in designing Unity Temple is the room inside. In the text of the *Autobiography*, "the room" in 1932 becomes "the great room" in 1943. The starting point for architecture is the "inner rhythm, deep planted," not surface, literature or symbol. The space in the great room is the "reality of the building." What is striking is that this room, the part of the building that he struggled with the most in 1906 and changed in detail even during construction, is put first in the order of importance in his narrative twenty-five years later.

Suggesting that the design began with the interior bestows a significance that the chronology of changes does not support. As his later notations on the drawings of the interior indicated, Wright tried to make that point, but in a strangely reverse way by saying the outside was coming in. If the starting point is the room inside, would not the continuity make the inside come out? Yet the goal to make the inside and outside continuous lies at the heart of an architecture derived from a Romantic desire for an embracing unity of all things.

In his description of Unity Temple in the first edition of *An Autobiography*, Wright explicitly eschews plastering or furring as part of the envelope. This is one indication why the Larkin Building was not an appropriate example for this architectural goal. Steel framing creates pockets and voids between structure and layers of enclosure. He takes these sentences out eleven years later, likely because Unity Temple is in fact plastered on the inside; the rough, "authentic" concrete does not appear in the interior, except as seen through the windows at the top of the walls, the viewpoint that Wright emphasized in the annotations he added in the 1930s to the 1906 perspectives. The concrete that does appear on the inside is finished in a dense smoothness that belies its rougher exterior appearance.

Wright repeats in various ways how he made Unity Temple original, natural, noble, "thoroughbred." He rejects "false facing," or "veneered Façade." He rejects the idea that one chooses a style. If it is anything, style is the natural consequence of creating a singular artifact by making all of its parts continuous. Layers, literature, style all frustrate architecture connecting to its origins. The word Wright would come to signify that origin was "nature."

The connecting link between mind and nature is geometry. This phenomenon is not quite like language, whose meanings are always subject to interpretation. A circle is the same in twentieth-century BCE Egypt as in twentieth-century Japan. In a rush of pure idealist philosophizing, Wright writes: "Reality is spirit—[the] essence brooding just behind [all] aspect. Seize it! And—after all [you will see the pattern of] reality is supergeometric." (This sentence is reworked in the second edition by the addition of words bracketed here to distinguish them.)

Geometry operates for an architect as an armature that transcends the foreground accumulation of human error. For Wright, radical and conservative are after the same thing in their pursuit of original truths. This pursuit characterizes America's calling as xxviii ∷ THE NOBLE ROOM

announced by Thomas Paine in the 1792 *Rights of Man*: "The case and circumstances of America present themselves as in the beginning of the world....We are...as if we had lived in the beginning of time." But Wright did not actually ignore the past. His response is more like one of his American icons, Walt Whitman, who begins his "Song of Myself" with the very delicate citation of the significance of past achievements when he writes: "Creeds and schools in abeyance, / Retiring back a while sufficed at what they are, never forgotten..." (lines 10–11).

Geometry is the "reality" that lies behind the variable surfaces according to Wright's essay on the "Japanese Print" of 1912, where he explicitly cites a Platonic precedent. He sees the Japanese printmaker approaching the world in much the same way. The printmaker does not show us a particular pine tree, but the "reality" of "pineness" through the characteristic geometric arrangement of its branches, needles, and position with respect to the ground (Wright 1992, 116–25). The prints he so avidly collected in the first decade of the twentieth century combined a complex representation of a three-dimensional scene and its two-dimensional pattern on the print's surface. That a surface could be both may have contributed to Wright's exploration of its potential in his own art of architecture.

Contemporary discussions at the turn of the twentieth century in nontraditional architectural circles were proposing a way to approach design not through precedent, but by use of what was called "pure design" (Frank 2008, 248–73). Was Wright addressing that discussion when he described his design process of Unity Temple in the following terms: "Design is abstraction of nature-elements in purely geometric terms—that is what we ought to call pure design" (Wright 1943, 157)? Using the patterns of geometric construction, architects could create buildings without relying on, particularly, Beaux Arts conventions.

Unity Temple intensifies these architectural traditions by being tightly strung on axes, symmetries, and volumetric hierarchies. It is the interior where Wright breaks free from that convention.

Wright was known to be very attentive to the world around him. He subscribed to leading design publications and, one almost gets the impression that while he paid attention to many things, it was mostly on the sly. Precedent was always involved, not as something whose quotation justified the work to those who think of culture as something compiled and curated, but as something to be consumed and digested; as nourishment for new growth. To even acknowledge that he paid attention to things around him ran the risk of being lumped into the academic view of architecture having no initiative itself and relying only on the authority of the past as justification. For Wright the past was nutrient, not credential.

The discussion that calls the building a "temple" is evidence of this effort to go back to origins. The congregation's pamphlet calls the new building the "temple," and Charles E. White, writing from Wright's Oak Park studio, refers to it as having "all the chaste beauty of a Greek temple" (Brooks 1981, 91).

The part of the design process of Unity Temple that Wright dramatizes in his narrative in the *Autobiography* is the problem of finding "concordance" between the Temple, or auditorium, part of Unity Temple, whose arrangement of formal parts was almost a given when the design began, and the secondary, secular part, Unity House. Finding that concordance, the making of an architectural whole out of different parts, was a conventional challenge. It was not the revolutionary challenge that the interior posed and about which Wright wrote almost nothing, except as a conclusion, not a search.

As Wright describes his labor, it took 34 studies to establish the formal continuity between the Temple and the House. "To establish harmony between these buildings of separate function proved difficult, utterly exasperating." Removing the phrase "harmony of the whole" from the later edition of *An Autobiography* aligns this later description with the 1908 first paper "In the Cause of Architecture" series, he uses Unity Temple as an example of various parts having their own formal expression in the whole: "This tendency to greater individuality of the parts emphasized by more and more complete articulation will be seen in the plans for Unity Church" (Wright 1992, 94).

Wright alternately values Unity Temple as an achievement that harmonized parts or as a demonstration of their discernable independence. With this concern Wright addresses only the volumetric disposition of the building. But the interior, the part that must have taken at least as many studies to arrive at a conclusion, is barely addressed. The conclusion that produced the desired concordance of parts was a known goal. The goal of the evolving continuity being sought in the interior was not yet clear. Maybe that is why he could not narrate its discovery. It would take Wright the rest of his career to explore that goal, find ways to construct it, and to encounter its limitations.

Precedents

There are precedents cited for Unity Temple, of course. I happen to think that Otto Wagner's Steinhoff church near Vienna, or the Secessionist gallery are not very convincing, if for no other reason than the form of Unity Temple is much closer to Wright's own Larkin Building and Unity Temple's auditorium block's insistent clarity all round contrasts with the residual appearance of the back of the Secessionist gallery. The geometric machinations of Otto Graf (1983) that emphasize the quadratic pattern seem to distract attention from the most fascinating aspect of the building, as do many other "analyses" (some partially based on Froebel block constructions), like those of Robert McCarter, Grant Manson, and others. To take Wright's volumetric conclusion as the focus of the analyses misses the possibility that this evidence of his mastery of geometric volumes was not, in fact, the major significance for Wright or for the stage of his career that Unity Temple represents.

The precedents in Wright's own work are clearer and focus on a central space that gave him the opportunity to explore the constructional requirements of that form. The drafting room (and the octagonal library) of his Oak Park Studio, 1895, only four blocks away from Unity Temple, used chains to suspend the floating balcony and solid corners to support the octagonal lantern. Its interior clearly expressed the structure, even celebrating it with the iron fittings linking the chains. The auditorium for his Uncle Jenkin Lloyd Jones's Lincoln Center of 1900 was projected to be a gathering space bound by four piers (brick covered steel like the Larkin Building) with bands of high windows lighting a space surrounded by balconies. The Hillside Home School built for his aunts in 1904, around the hill from where Taliesin would be built nine years later, was a further exploration of the centralized space with solid corners and a "floating" balcony. In all these examples, the tradition of making the architecture out of the elements of construction is fully visible.

The most historically challenging "precedent" was once thought to be the Yahara Boat House in Madison, Wisconsin. Through the brilliant and fortuitous sleuthing of Jack Holzhueter at the Wisconsin Historical Society, we now know that this stunning project was actually designed simultaneously with Unity Temple, not in 1902 as Wright represented it. Holzhueter (1989, 163–96) suggests that the visit to Japan made in the spring 1905, between the Larkin Building, Unity Temple, and Yahara Boat House, contributed to the significant advance in Wright's architecture. Seeing an architectural convention in Japan that consisted of planes rather than volumes (a characteristic of Japanese architecture identified much later as "ma," or interval, by Guenter Nitschke and by the Japanese architect Arata Isozaki [2001]) along with Wright's increasing appreciation of the wood block print, may have initiated a new way of seeing continuity as an exploration of planar development, which unfolds in the Unity Temple interior.

The masterful massing and distribution of volumes are the most visible aspects of the design of Unity Temple. Its uncompromising geometric clarity; its recesses and projections, the sheer aggressiveness of all those right-angled corners created the "plasticity" remarked on by foreign visitors like Cornelius van de Ven, who "defined that phenomenon quite remarkably as the 'three-dimensional' " (1978, 231). The third dimension is a characteristic Wright himself emphasized at various times. The evolution of the block, which Unity Temple so evidently seems to be, into the "slab" as the alternative to the pointed arch or spire and the dome creates the three-dimensionality that Wright valued so highly.

But the implied solidity of the "block of sculptured building material" contradicted the inner space. The interior had to be open, not opaque, and one way Wright connected plasticity and interior space in the same conception was to describe Unity Temple as "screened" by the concrete "monoliths." One imagines the stones of Stonehenge gathered more tightly together, marking off an interior with the slits between them like the fissures in Unity Temple's exterior. The use of the word "screen" to describe those brooding, dark concrete walls, tries to overcome the impact of their solidity and geometric compactness with a word that suggests surfaces that can, in fact, be folded.

Two and Three Dimensions

In the 1925 essay "In the Cause of Architecture: The Third Dimension," Wright places Unity Temple in the sequence of his career's development. It is another stage in his continual repositioning of Unity Temple, as he will do a decade later in *An Autobiography* and in subsequent references. In 1925 he writes:

> Unity Temple asserts again the quality and value of the third dimension in asserting the form within to be the essential to find expression. The reinforced concrete slab as a new architectural expression, is here used for its own sake as "Architecture." This building is a cast monolith. A transition building as it is, wherein the character of the wooden forms or boxes, necessary at this time in casting concrete construction are made a virtue of the whole in "style": that

process of construction made a conscious aesthetic feature of the whole. Its "style" is due to the way it was "made." A sense of the third dimension in the use of the "box" and the "slab"—and a sense of the room within as the thing to be expressed in arranging them are what made Unity Temple; instead of the two-dimension-sense of the traditional block mass sculptured into architectural form from without (1925, 209–214).

Wright is apparently trying to describe a very complicated relationship between two and three dimensions. The "box" and the "slab" are three-dimensional while the "block mass" is not. How can this be? The last phrase in the quotation that identifies the sculptured block with two dimensions seems contradictory on the face of it. Two years earlier, writing about the Imperial Hotel in Tokyo, Wright tried to be more direct: "I am not one of those who conceive of a building as a carved and sculpted block of building material. This is two-dimension thinking" (1992, 178). Maybe the issue is that architecture has been considered primarily as a façade; a view of architecture that emphasizes the exterior wall of a building as a text promoting the interests of the powers that built edifices along the city's streets. The tradition of representing architecture through these two-dimensional drawings, so effectively distributed in the Renaissance through printed books by the likes of Palladio, among others, had implications that Wright was trying to overcome.

In the chapter "This Will Kill That," from *Notre Dame de Paris*, Victor Hugo steps outside the narrative about Esmerelda and the bell-ringer Quasimodo to present his version of the history of architecture and the destructive impact of printing on architecture. He foretold the substitution of the ubiquitous printed book, seen as a flock of birds, for the weighty, unique edifice, seen as a mountain. Wright read this analysis before coming to Chicago, and I believe it became a central challenge for the aspiring architect to answer. Architecture for a democratic America would be in the

Figure 8. The Usonian house, designed some thirty years after Unity Temple, is the clearest achievement of the folded plane as structure with its two-and-a-half-inch wood walls, whose strips of different woods show visual, as well as constructional, continuity. Photo courtesy Sidney K. Robinson

possession of each person, not just the privileged few. The folded plane of the book's page would be transformed into the folded planes of Wright's Usonian houses' walls designed in the 1930s (fig. 8). The complex relation Wright is trying to clarify between two and three dimensions may also be an attempt to reduce the weight, the costly solidity of the architecture of edifices by substituting the more economical plasticity of the folded plane.

Unity Temple may be seen as the opening skirmish in Wright's life-long quest to build architecture that maintained the primary virtue of "plasticity," but left behind its traditional source in favor of a much more accessible manifestation through the folded plane. Going even farther, it could signal Wright's final triumph of architecture over literature. One cannot be sure, but the interior of Unity Temple surely challenges tradition as found both in history and in its own concrete walls.

The volumetric arrangement of the building is clearly not the result of the material, which began as brick. The concrete is more important because of its implications for the interior. The very absence of the need to assemble constructional parts, made possible by the continuity of the reinforced concrete, suggests a continuity of enclosing plane that the light-colored plaster and the wood stripping sought to reinforce.

When H.R. Hitchcock, in his book *In the Nature of Materials* (1941), refers to the wood stripping in Unity Temple's interior as "structural as well," one cannot be sure whether he is suggesting that its linearity recalls more traditional placement of structural members or whether he really understood that "the fold" is here being presented as a new structural possibility. It is precisely the freedom from structural assemblage that suggests the flowing continuity wrapping heretofore separate elements into a singularity. However, Wright chooses to emphasize the more traditional assemblage of "monoliths" as his achievement at Unity Temple even as he points out the importance of the "great room." The three-dimensional potential of the folded plane rather than the obvious tradition of the solid block is what Wright began to explore on the interior of Unity Temple. His attack on the thin planarity of the European modernists, particularly the ones with whom he shared the walls of Hitchcock and Johnson's "International Style" exhibit in 1932 at the Museum of Modern Art: Mies, Gropius, Le Corbusier, was based on their lack of the prized "plasticity." He was making a crucial distinction with the interior of Unity Temple: it is "plastic" and planar at once.

The divergence between inside and out is present in earlier Oak Park studio work, but not to this degree. Even when the exterior is masonry, as in the Barton house 1903 in Buffalo, and the interior is plaster divided by wood stripping, the patterns of that stripping abstractly reinforce a tectonic pattern; they outline, reinforce, and parallel the placement of structural elements. The Prairie houses almost universally use the wood stripping in this fashion.

The patterns are applied, of course, but they are derived from an abstraction of load-bearing or spanning elements of construction. The singular departure of the interior of Unity Temple is how it obscures structural patterns that began in the assembly of constructional elements and were merged through the use of poured concrete. When the Prairie houses have a plaster exterior, of course, the connection between inside plaster and exterior plaster creates a direct continuity, and there are tentative forays into wood stripping folding around corners.

The Interior

Is Unity Temple's interior a three-dimensional entity describable as a sculpted void, or is it a space created by a continuously folded, articulated plane? Unity Temple's interior is the "transition" stage where Wright began to move from the tradition of the former to the revolutionary implications of the latter.

As we have seen, Wright redesigned the interior of Unity Temple in a sequence that moved away from a more traditional constructional expression to a demonstration of planar continuity. The wood stripping is a "graphic" technique he used to explore this goal of continuity suggested by the continuous concrete material that was both enclosure and structure. His changes in the location of some of the stripping even during construction reinforces his continuing search for the potential of this new approach. Wright was walking a fine line by making an interior of folded planes while at the same time asserting that surfaces of "façades" and veneers were fatal substitutes for solid truths. "Plasticity" could be achieved not only by solidity, but by folds in screens that were not surfaces. This distinction is not trivial or Wright just pulling a fast one. A surface is "on" something; it is not itself. A screen is a thing itself and therefore can contribute to a vision of an architecture that is unified and integral.

Standing in the "great room," one cannot miss the pattern of the wood stripping as it wraps around various corners. Rather than outlining the separate constructional "blocks" that gather around the space, they obscure them by tying them together. The most compelling demonstration of this goal appears at the crucial tops of the piers. There the abacus block is a structural and visual transition from the ceiling to the pier, but the stripping that would have completed the pattern if the ceiling had been free to continue is bent around it. The planar pattern overlaps, even absorbs the structural element. Around almost every corner of vertical or horizontal architectural element, a plane outlined by the wood stripping is folded. The previous outlining of structural elements by panels of stripping is maintained only on the outer, concrete walls. These elements, part of the more conventional axial, geometric constructional goals of the exterior, therefore, signal their exterior significance by the clear framing that contrasts to the folding of the purely interior elements.

The sequence entering the auditorium from the narthex or vestibule begins with the blank, predominantly gray tones of the wall to the auditorium. The gray is a continuation of the exterior concrete, with flat panels outlined by stripping. At the first turn, the lighter yellow tone appears as an outlined panel, and the next turn into the main space in the low, dark passages at a level below the main floor opens to the light-toned, brightly lit auditorium. One is prepared for the impact of the significant contrast between inside and out in incremental stages. The smooth plaster, the light colors, and the flat bands of dark wood transform the weight and solidity of the concrete into a thin membrane wrapping all faces of the structural elements, at once dematerializing them and weaving them into a complex, continuously folded plane. This is the revolution, the transubstantiation of conventional construction into a new vision of spatial, structural, and conceptual continuity.

Wright had announced this new direction in his talk "The Art and Craft of the Machine" (1901) at Hull House some five years before he began working on Unity Temple's interior. At the beginning of the lecture, he makes a prophetic distinction between the old form of art and, by implication, the new:

> Art in the grand old sense—meaning Art in the sense of
> structural tradition, whose craft is fashioned upon the
> handicraft idea, ancient or modern; an art wherein this
> form and that form as structural parts were laboriously
> joined in such a way as to beautifully emphasize the man-
> ner of the joining; the million and one ways of beautifully
> satisfying bare structural necessities, which have come
> down to us chiefly through the books as "Art" (1992,
> 58–69).

His analysis of the "old art" is well developed, just like the volumetric achievement of Unity Temple, while the characterization
of the "new art" is haltingly suggested in subsequent phrases
throughout the lecture, very much like the halting advances in the
design of Unity Temple's interior. In the lecture, this distinction
between "new" and "old" gets tangled up with "the machine," the
ostensible subject of his challenge to the Arts and Crafts Society.
Wright uses words like "simple, sincere clothing of plastic material
that idealizes its purpose without structural pretense…that the plastic art may live…plastic treatment—a pliant, sympathetic treatment
of its needs that the body of structural precedent cannot yield."
Admittedly these fragments do not give a clear definition, but by
turning the description of the old art on its head, we do get a better definition. And in the interior of Unity Temple we see the first
architectural (mainly graphic) demonstration of what the new art
would become, as structure is transformed into plastic continuity.

One is struck by the fact that this architectural "advance" is
achieved through strips of oak and paint! What other Wright building can one name where paint is so critical to the effect? For a brief
moment, one might imagine that Wright approaches the marvel of,
forgive me, the transformations achieved in Rococo interiors.

And yet, at the same time, Wright has produced a stunning
example of the volumetric, axial, hierarchy of traditional architecture in the body of Unity Temple. Its "quadratic" formal evolution,

its intriguing motival differentiation, its brilliant working out of interlocking solids and voids, which the Yale architectural historian Vincent Scully (1961, 31) marveled was Wright's particular genius, makes Unity Temple satisfying in more classical terms. The Dutch architect Berlage even goes so far as to see that in Unity Temple "something of the classical temple is revived" (1938, 35).

In a building designed more than four decades later, Wright was able finally to construct the continuity and plasticity that in Unity Temple were "merely" wood strips and paint. The Guggenheim Museum (fig. 9) in New York (1945), a two-part composition entered between the major elements, with a sky-lit, balconied central space, finally substitutes bands of balcony fronts and ramped recesses for oak strips and yellow paint! The continuity of its

Figure 9. The Guggenheim Museum in New York is the ultimate achievement of the structural and visual continuity only suggested by the stripping inside Unity Temple.

concrete construction uniting enclosure and structure actually achieves the result only hinted at in Oak Park. Its finishing coating successfully, some would say disturbingly, dematerializes any sense of construction in favor of a smooth continuity. It is almost as if the concrete fortification that protects Unity Temple's folded interior membrane has been chiseled away to expose the tender surface of the museum's billowing insides. Finally the interior has become the exterior, even at the risk of exposing its vulnerability. The Guggenheim is Wright's total architectural realization both as a plastic volume and as a structural ideal; a culmination of the ideas he was only able to suggest, or approximate forty years earlier in the interior of Unity Temple.

As we began this foreword with the proposition that Wright started with tradition, reinterpreted it, and then created something new within, we now have a more complete understanding of just how deeply this exploration of future architectural concepts is embedded in the architecture of Unity Temple. It is simultaneously a successful composition of the old art and a triumphant overture to the new.

—Sidney K. Robinson
Taliesin
2008

ACKNOWLEDGMENTS

Every book is the responsibility of the author, but there are always many people who have made the book possible. This volume is not only no exception to that rule, but the author has the added obligation to thank people who contributed to its creation or encouraged the project, over a long period of years.

A great debt is owed to the Unity Temple Restoration Foundation: for access to records; for support in the original grant for photographs; to the several directors of the Foundation over the years, most especially Emily Roth and former director Keith Bringe, for their belief in and enthusiasm for the project; to long-ago members Carol Kelm, William B. Fyfe, Barbara Ballinger, Bob Bell, Peg Zak, Lyman Shephard, and Jeannette Fields, as well as recent supporters of the book, Eric O'Malley and Rick Smith. The Unitarian Universalist Congregation in Oak Park has been behind this project for many years, and former minister Jay Deacon helped the author clarify ideas. Various congregants have helped in a variety of ways: Bill Crozier, Bob Compton, Ron Moline, David Siegel, and others who have moved on and whose names have, unfortunately, been lost.

Professor David Van Zanten, of Northwestern University, read an early draft and provided thoughtful and helpful comments and suggestions.

The staff at the Oak Park Library and the Historical Society of Oak Park & River Forest also have been of great assistance.

The Graham Foundation supported the project with a grant to subsidize the gathering of images from the Frank Lloyd Wright Foundation, and the staff at Taliesin have been helpful in getting images for the project.

Sidney Robinson's contributions are varied and immeasurable, and the enthusiasm, organizational skills, and dedication of Alex Lubertozzi and Jennifer Barrell have moved this project toward completion in time for the centennial of the dedication of Unity Temple.

My profound thanks are extended to all of them.

THE NOBLE ROOM

THE FIRST IDEA WAS
TO KEEP A NOBLE ROOM
FOR WORSHIP IN MIND.

FRANK LLOYD WRIGHT

INTRODUCTION

Frank Lloyd Wright's Unity Temple, the home of the Unitarian Universalist Congregation in Oak Park, Illinois, is one of the best-known and frequently illustrated buildings of the twentieth century and would, probably by consensus, be deemed a major monument in the history of American and even world architecture.

The building is visited by tens of thousands each year; its great acoustics make it a much-desired venue for professional musicians; the beauty of its interior makes it much sought after for social, religious, and charitable events by people of a wide variety of backgrounds. The building is not large, though the combination of its massing and the concrete construction give it a dignity and presence that makes it seem larger than it really is. But, once one is inside, the experience of light, color, and the exquisiteness of the geometry place the visitor in another world, and that is the source of Wright's genius.

Justly famous for its innovations both in design and technique, and widely appreciated on a purely aesthetic basis, it was characterized by Wright as his best early building and has been mentioned and praised by hundreds of writers. Clearly, Wright thought of this building as one of the most important of his career, and the summation of the ideas to which he was attracted in his early years, saying, "Unity Temple makes an entirely new architecture," and, "When I finished Unity Temple, I had it. I knew I had the beginning of a great thing, a great truth in architecture. Now architecture could be free."[1] Yet, for all its worldwide fame, it has been discussed in detail by few.

Even during Wright's lifetime, and certainly from Grant C. Manson's pioneering critical study *Frank Lloyd Wright to 1910: The First Golden Age* published the year before the architect died in 1959, through the popular biography *Many Masks: A Life of Frank Lloyd Wright*, by Brendan Gill, published in 1987, both scholars and popularizers alike have relied all too heavily on Wright's *An Autobiography*. They have accepted the author's description in the chapter, "Designing Unity Temple," as both literal and factual, ignoring both Wright's obvious disinterest in historical narrative and his disinclination to share the limelight with others who may have had a significant role in any of his projects. As Joseph Siry put it so aptly in his 1996 monograph on the building, "So successful was Wright in fixing the terms of discussion about his own architecture that the shifts in his accounts over time have often been left unexamined."[2] They have compounded this error in two ways; they have consulted the edition of 1943 (usually in the form of a later reprint) rather than the less widely available but somewhat more revealing first edition of 1932, and they have failed to check the accuracy of the architect's statements against other appropriate sources. And, surprisingly, even those authors such as Gill, who were aware of Wright's tendency to create history in order to show off his unquestioned abilities—this original and innovative genius—in the most favorable light, appear never to have confirmed the supposed "facts" with as much as an examination of the local Oak Park newspapers or the extensive pictorial archives of the Frank Lloyd Wright Memorial Foundation at Taliesin. Only after introducing the subject in an article and then in his monograph, *Unity Temple: Frank Lloyd Wright and Architecture for Liberal Religion*, of 1996, did

Joseph Siry explore the theological underpinnings of the building's design.[3] Yet, in spite of his scrupulous utilization of the original documents, there is still no detailed examination of the day-by-day and blow-by-blow account of the creation of this great and inspiring building.

It is, therefore, the intention of this book to examine this important national landmark, Unity Temple, from both artistic and historical perspectives, and to document the paths to its construction and reception. In addition to utilizing unpublished and never-before-quoted correspondence of the building committee for the new church and the minutes of the board of trustees and various other documents in Unity Temple's archives, Wright's own words shall be examined, and we shall attempt to understand how and why he chose to write the distorted but extremely important seven-page chapter of *An Autobiography*. And Wright was to reference Unity Temple over and again in his writings, noting only two years before his death, "Here came the poetic principle of freedom itself as a new revelation in architecture. This new freedom that was first consciously demonstrated in Unity Temple, Oak Park."[4] In trying to understand the genesis of this great building, design, technical, economic, and human factors will be explored, and, hopefully, we can emerge with a new and more complete view as to the sources of Wright's design and its importance in the history of both American and modern architecture.

CHAPTER I

UNITY CHURCH TO 1905

A t about 5:00 A.M. on the morning of June 4, 1905, a violent thunderstorm hit the village of Oak Park, Illinois, and one of the many bolts of lightning that dramatically lit up the sky hit the steeple of the Unity Church. The steeple soon came crashing down, and the entire wooden structure fell to the flames; within a short time, it was completely destroyed. From the ashes of this local tragedy was to spring one of the great architectural achievements of the early twentieth century.

Unity Church, the predecessor of Oak Park's Unity Temple, had been founded on January 25, 1871, when eleven Unitarian- and Universalist-oriented members of the Union Church met in the home of E. W. Hoard to discuss the formation of a new and liberal organization. There were already several congregations and at least one freestanding Sunday school in the area comprising both present-day Oak Park and the Austin area of Chicago to the east, and many people were loosely affiliated with and supported more than one of the struggling religious institutions. This was especially true of the business and civic leaders in the adjacent communities of Oak Park and Ridgeland (now joined together as Oak Park), as they thought it important to have strong and viable institutions to attract settlers who would buy their land and purchase from the businesses they controlled.

Though the Union Church leaned toward the most liberal form of Protestant worship and governance, the group who held this organizational meeting had become increasingly uncomfortable with the direction being taken by their eight-year-old congregation, as it moved from an evangelical but non-denominational institution toward a closer identification with the established Congregational denomination of Protestantism.[1] And, when it appeared that Union Church might actually affiliate with the Congregationalists, those committed to a more liberal form of belief felt it was time to act. At that first organizational meeting, an amount in excess of $5,000 was pledged toward the construction of a church, and within a week the fledgling congregation had adopted both a constitution and by-laws, and taken the name Unity Church of Oak Park. The first board of trustees was elected at a special meeting on March 1, with Edwin O. Gale (fig. 10), an astute and successful businessman, as treasurer, and with the selection of a five-member building committee.[2]

One of the members of the committee was Milton C. Niles, a large landowner who played a pivotal role in the location and funding of the new church building. It was decided to build the church near the southwest corner of Wisconsin Avenue (now Marion) and Pleasant Streets, close to the Harlem stop on the railroad. The group agreed to purchase a lot from Niles: he then donated the adjacent piece of property to the church, a fact that must have influenced the decision in favor of that location at least as much as the proximity to the railroad station, for there was a lot of open land in the area. Construction began almost immediately, a minister was hired, and the church was completed in just over a year and dedicated on August 11, 1872. The church was a traditional Gothic Revival structure (fig. 11) of one floor, with neither side-aisles nor a crossing, but with a tall steeple at the entrance end and with engaged buttresses between each bay. The name of the architect is lost, but it is known

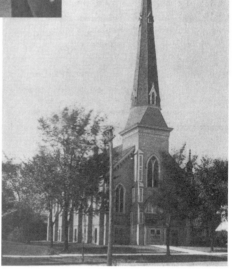

Figure 10. Edwin O. Gale's family were early settlers in the area. He was a founding member of Unity Church, its first treasurer, and he sold the property to the congregation upon which Unity Temple was built. Courtesy The Historical Society of Oak Park & River Forest

Figure 11. The original Unity Church, dedicated in August of 1872, was a one-story Gothic-style building with a steeple, on the southwest corner of Wisconsin (now Marion Street) and Pleasant in Oak Park. Edwin Gale donated almost half the cost of construction. Courtesy Unity Temple Restoration Foundation

that the total cost of land and construction came to $13,869 with $5,600 of the total donated by the treasurer Gale.[3]

The congregation experienced some difficult years at first, for several reasons. First, many of the church's most important backers had suffered materially as a result of the Chicago Fire, and few of the members could be described as being among the really wealthy families in town. Then, too, as a loosely knit association of less-than-traditional Unitarians and a group of Universalists, even less committed to a highly developed structure, the congregation had neither the type of institutional support provided by a normal institutional affiliation nor the status offered by identification with one of the mainstream churches. Another problem related to the lack of a clear denominational focus was highlighted when the first minister left under duress, in a little over one year, and was replaced by one ordained in the Unitarian Church. There were several more changes in religious leadership in the next decade, underscoring the lack of identity and purpose of the congregation. To provide some structure and a minimal identification with the larger block within the congregation, the Universalists, a Church within Unity Church was organized in 1882. The membership in that more structured body was recognized by the Universalist denomination, but the church itself (hereafter known as the "parish"), succeeded in remaining free of direct institutional affiliation without alienating the Unitarians in the group and managed to be open to all interested in liberal religion.[4] That solution set the pattern for the future of the congregation, and though there was a merger of the Unitarians and the Universalists at a national level, almost one hundred years later, Unity Temple is still known as one of the most liberal and least dedicated to dogma among religious organizations.

The selection of Augusta Chapin (1836–1905), an energetic, multitalented and highly organized Universalist woman, as pastor in 1886, helped redirect the energies of the congregation, and a period of growth ensued. This remarkable person (fig. 12) had been preaching since 1859, had been ordained in the Universalist ministry in 1863 (only the second woman to receive ordination), and had held pulpits in Michigan, Iowa, Pennsylvania, and two others in Illinois before accepting the position in Oak Park. She was also the first woman in the United States to be awarded the

Figure 12. Augusta Chapin was the minister of Unity Church from 1886 to 1892. A friend of both Frank Lloyd Wright's mother and his minister uncle, Jenkin Lloyd Jones, she was the first woman in the United States to be awarded the doctor of divinity degree. Courtesy Unity Temple Restoration Foundation

degree of doctor of divinity. Later in life, again breaking new ground for women in the ministry and education, she was to serve as an extension lecturer for both Lombard College and the University of Chicago, and to have a leadership role in the Women's Committee of the Columbian Exposition. In addition, Chapin was active in the Temperance movement and other reform organizations, and was an active participant in the affairs of the Universalist organization.[5]

Among those who joined the church during the six years of her pastorate, there were two without whom this story could not be told. The first was Edwin H. Ehrman (fig. 13) who joined in 1889 and was later to play a critical role in the construction of Unity Temple, and who remained an active member of the congregation for the next half-century. The other was an old friend of Reverend Chapin, Anna Jones Wright, the mother of Frank Lloyd

Wright, who, together with her son and younger daughter, briefly boarded with Chapin and who was to begin her spotty affiliation with Unity Church in 1890.[6] Anna Wright was the sister of Jenkin Lloyd Jones, the minister of All Soul's Unitarian Church in Chicago (1882–1905), a leader of the more radical branch of Unitarianism in his position of director of the Western Unitarian Conference (1875–1884) and an associate of the Unity Church minister in a variety of liberal causes. Anna's ex husband, William Cary Wright (1825–1904), had started his ministerial career as a Baptist, but had later preached as a Unitarian minister within the same conference as his brother-in-law Jenkin. Thus, the relations between Reverend Chapin and her boarders were built on both strong religious and familial ties.

Reverend Chapin resigned her position in 1891, actually leaving the congregation in 1892, and went on to have an important leadership role at the World Parliament of Religions held in

Figure 13. Edwin H. Ehrman, a member of Unity Church since 1889, was a local whose life was bound up with Oak Park and the Church. The factory manager and corporate secretary of Chicago Screw Company, he chaired both the church and grounds and the building committee during construction of the new church. Courtesy Unity Temple Restoration Foundation

conjunction with the Columbian Exposition in Chicago in 1893. She chaired the Women's Committee, addressed both the opening and closing sessions of the Parliament, and was the only woman to chair a session of the Parliament. Clearly, she was a woman with rather strong views about the roles women should have within the church, and it is tempting to think about what the young Frank Lloyd Wright must have heard and learned while living in her home. Certainly, in an era when people sat and talked at the dinner table, uninterrupted by either phone calls or television programs, he must have heard quite a bit about the equality of the sexes, the ability of women to lead, and—probably—about the ways church architecture and design supported the patriarchal system. Further, Reverend Chapin was already a much-traveled person, throughout the United States and in Europe, and had served a variety of congregations, from New York and Boston to San Francisco and the Northwest. The young Wright had traveled nowhere outside of the Midwest when he resided in her home, and it is easy to speculate about the churches and other civic buildings that she must have described to the budding architect who had only seen such buildings in books or in the form of engravings. And, perhaps of the greatest potential importance for the impact on the future Unity Temple, one of Chapin's greatest accomplishments in fighting patriarchy within the Church was the adoption of her proposal for non-gender-specific wording in the rules adopted at the Universalist Centennial Celebration of 1870, at which she served as the minister delegate representing the state of Iowa.

When Chapin left the congregation and Oak Park, she was followed by Dr. Rodney F. Johonnot (fig. 14), a man who had resigned his position as minister of the First Universalist Church of Lewistown, Maine, to accept the $1,800-per-year pulpit in Oak Park. By 1896, the twenty-fifth anniversary of the founding of the congregation, attendance at services had reached an all-time high of 225, and the membership had responded positively to the ambitious lecture and publication programs initiated by Chapin and

Figure 14. Reverend Dr. Rodney F. Johonnot had served in a Universalist Church in Lewistown, Maine, before coming to Oak Park and had ties to both the Universalist and Unitarian parts of the congregation. He served as minister from 1892 to 1910, leaving at the height of his popularity. Courtesy The Historical Society of Oak Park & River Forest

continued and developed by her successor. The Sunday school also grew, making it obvious that the lack of sufficient secondary space was becoming a fairly severe problem for the congregation.

Dr. Johonnot, a dynamic administrator and effective organizer, soon suggested that the building was not only insufficient for the needs of the growing parish and its programs, but was also getting to be old enough to require replacement.[7] The idea that the age of the structure contributed to the desire to replace it has often been repeated, though it is difficult to imagine why a thirty-year-old church building should be perceived as old enough to warrant replacement. However, it seems clear that one major issue is the need for classrooms, and storage and so on, in a congregation oriented toward the education of their children. Another reason might have been liturgical, and it may be that the liturgical issues that arose in planning a new building were really the important ones that the minister wanted to address. In any event, Dr. Johonnot was insistent about the need for a new building, and in 1901 a new church building fund was established by the unanimous vote of the parish at the annual meeting of March 25, 1901; special collections were to be taken both at Christmas and Easter, each year, with the receipts earmarked for the new building. Contributions were extremely modest for the next few years, with few strongly committed to contributing to a building fund geared to construction in the unspecified future. Thus, at the end of 1904, the board of trustees, probably acting upon the suggestion of their minister, sent the following solicitation letter as part of a Christmas appeal:

To the Friends of Unity Church:

At the annual parish meeting March 25, 1901, it was unanimously voted to create a New Church Building Fund and to take special collections for this purpose on Christmas and Easter of each year.

The present edifice is the oldest church building in Oak Park having been built thirty years ago. While a splendid monument to the devotion of the members of that day, it is not adequate for all our present needs nor does it represent present ideas of church architecture.

To hold our own in the line of progress, to increase our usefulness and attract new people, to make ourselves an enduring force in this community lays on us the necessity for a new edifice. Up to the present time no effort has been made to do more than create the nucleus of a Building Fund; but together with the Birthday Fund which is devoted to the same purpose we now have on hand $814.63. It now seems time to endeavor to obtain a larger offering than heretofore that the Fund may begin to take on adequate proportions. With a growing fund we are likely to receive bequests and other donations.

We therefore ask that a generous offering be made this Christmas season. Instead of the customary dime, give a dollar, instead of the usual dollar give five, instead of the usual five, send a check for twenty-five. When we remember that one church in this village gives several thousand dollars to its building fund each Easter, may we not expect an offering of at least some hundred dollars? This can be realized if all will be willing to make some sacrifice for the future church. The children and youths should take a special interest.

A generous offering will make all happy and fill us with hope for the future. Continuing thus, in ten years we shall be justified in beginning on the erection of an edifice which shall be both beautiful and permanent. This is an opportunity for making a Christmas present to the church.

The letter was signed by the six members of the board and dated December 1904.[8] An interesting and important point in the letter, perhaps included in passing, is the comment about the current building being out of step with current ideas in church architecture. As it was a perfectly conventional building for its time, the comment might have significance in terms of ongoing questions about both the structure of the church and the structure of churches, then still being debated in the Universalist camp.

A few months after the Christmas letter was circulated, at the thirty-fifth annual meeting of the parish society held on March 27, 1905, "a general discussion followed in regard to the building of a new church. On motion of Mr. Ehrman, seconded by Mrs. Sturtevant, the board of trustees was authorized at its discretion to call a meeting to discuss fully the problem of building a new church."[9] This is the first time that we see the name of Ehrman taking a position in regard to a new church building, but the man could never have dreamed of what lay in store for him over the next four years.

The meeting was called two months later, as a Special Congregational Meeting on May 24, at Unity Church, chaired by the new president of the congregation, Thomas J. Skillin (fig. 15) and with the agenda devoted exclusively to the subject of a new church building. After reading the resolution that had provided

Figure 15. Thomas J. Skillin was a very active man in the Village of Oak Park, serving on the school board and as the president of Unity Church at the time of the fire. Wright presents him as a "doubting Thomas" but notes his call of congratulations after the building was dedicated. Courtesy The Historical Society of Oak Park & River Forest

the authorization for the special meeting, and outlining the issues before the parish, Mr. Skillin opened the floor for discussion. Some members thought that the present building was inadequate, some felt that it met the current needs of the parish, and some were sufficiently negative to suggest that the congregation's future was uncertain and to wonder if they might not soon be facing a situation in which there would be no Unity Church. After a free-wheeling exchange of ideas, the president was asked for his assessment as to the physical condition of the church, the structural soundness of the timbers under the Sunday school room floor, the condition of the spire, and that of the roof, etc. Further discussion ensued until Mrs. Nash, one of those who favored a new building, rose to call for pledges to support the construction of a new church. Those most vocal in support of the plan, including the minister, the president, and J.H. Heald Jr., immediately offered pledges. Others, whether in favor of a new building or not, thought such an emotional and dramatic response to be imprudent and discouraged further pledging at that time.

Mr. Adams moved that it be the sense of this meeting that
a new church building be erected if possible and that a
committee of five be appointed by the President and the
Board to investigate Ways Means and Possibilities and
report at a special meeting of the Parish to be called by the
board of trustees. Unanimously carried. Mr. Lewis moved
that this committee be requested to report before the summer vacation. Carried.[10]

H.A. Taylor, C.A. Sharpe, John Lewis, Dwight Jackson, and
W.G. Adams were appointed that same evening. The minister, as a
leader of the new church forces, was delighted, and he preached a
sermon on the next Sunday, "The Place and Work of Unity
Church," as a positive response to those who were pessimistic about
the future of the congregation.

However, Dr. Johonnot's efforts and those first steps taken by
the new ways and means committee were mooted the very next
Sunday when lightning struck the church at Pleasant and Wisconsin, and the building was totally destroyed by the ensuing fire
(fig. 16). James H. Heald Jr., one of those who had been quick to
make a financial pledge at the special meeting, lived across the
street from the church and had witnessed its destruction. He
penned so graphic a description of the event that it is well worth
repeating verbatim:

On Sunday, June 4, 1905, I was partially awakened about
5 o'clock in the morning by several loud peals of thunder
and violent downpouring of rain. The rain subsided somewhat and I remember hearing a noise which I supposed to
be water dropping off the eaves of the house next door and
I remember thinking what a violent rain it must have been
to cause water enough to fall and sound like that. Suddenly
my mother called to me "Unity Church is on fire!" Quickly
springing out of bed, I ran to our west window where the

steeple of the church could be seen blazing like a huge torch. The noise which I had supposed to have been made by falling water, was the crackling of the fire.... How I got my clothes on I do not know, but my brothers and I were among the first to arrive. The fire department had just arrived and was making vain efforts to throw water on the fire in the blazing steeple. The pressure of the water, however, was totally inadequate and it was evident they would be unable to reach the fire in the steeple, but it seemed certain that they could prevent it from spreading to the main building. The boys and young men present felt that they must do something and so the rear door leading to the Sunday School was broken open and the pianos, Sunday School tables, chairs, etc. were carried out and placed in a shed at the rear of the church.

The blazing steeple fell to the ground with a great crash, and fire seemed instantly to spread to all parts of the building. The stained glass windows melted and ran out of their frames and our dear old church building was a mass of flames. I have always regarded the day of the Unity Church fire as the most exciting day of my life. Providence had decided we must have a new church building.[11]

Additional details concerning the fire were carried in the next Saturday's edition of the local weekly, the *Oak Leaves*, under the title "Unity Church Fire." The story reported that the night switchman at the elevated terminal at Harlem Avenue had seen the flames and had activated the fire alarm at the corner. It was also noted that the lightning had knocked out phone service in the area, making it impossible for those who first saw the fire to reach the fire department by telephone. The article elaborated on young Heald's story, informing the readers how the firemen turned their attention to the neighboring homes and the Baptist church on the other side of Wisconsin Avenue, the roof of the latter having caught fire by

Figure 16. Unity Church burned to the ground after lightning hit the steeple in the early morning of June 4, 1905. It was a total loss, with only a piano and some of the classroom furnishings saved. From the disaster came the inspiration for a different sort of structure. Courtesy The Historical Society of Oak Park & River Forest

that time. It was mentioned that burning embers were carried for several blocks, due to the high winds that had accompanied the storm, and that it was believed that only the heavy rains and the wet buildings saved the community from further destruction that night. The building was a total loss, along with all the auditorium's furniture and furnishings. The piano, chairs, dishes, and silverware that belonged to the ladies' society and used for entertainments, and several paintings were all that was saved.[12]

Coincidentally, the regular monthly meeting of the board of trustees was scheduled for the day that the church burned, and that meeting was held in the home of President Skillin that very morning. The minutes indicate that "messages of sympathy and offers of the use of their own places of worship" had already been received from the First Congregational Church, the Baptist Church, the First Presbyterian Church, and even Nakama and Kenilworth Halls, two privately controlled facilities.[13] Support came from outside the community as well, as evidenced by this note sent to the minister the day after the fire: "Enclosed please find check for $27.11 being the collection taken at the St. Paul's Universalist Sunday school last Sunday and voted to be sent to you on account of your recent loss."[14] The board members asked the minister to respond to all the expressions of goodwill and to work with the president to select a place for the future services of the parish. Mr. Skillin was also charged with contacting their insurer about a financial settlement, and he was asked to schedule a special meeting of the entire parish. That meeting was scheduled for the following Friday evening and was held at the First Baptist Church, just across the street from their own destroyed building. At the meeting the (to the modern reader) amazing news that the insurance claim had already been adjusted was made, and they were notified that the parish would receive almost all of the $9,500 insurance carried on the old church building. It was also noted that several small amounts had already been offered toward the building of a new church, and the names and amounts of the donations were read to the audience. Mr. Taylor gave an informal report of the ways and means committee's activities before the fire rendered them obsolete. He also formally moved that the parish proceed toward the construction of a new building, and that was approved unanimously. The parish also mandated the board to appoint four small committees: ways and means, site, plans, and building. The minutes of the meeting make no mention of a discussion about the site, but the next morning's edition of the *Oak Leaves* noted that:

> The decision to appoint a committee on site is the result of
> the well nigh unanimous opinion of the membership that
> the new building ought not to be in the old location, but
> that it should be in some place more central and where it
> will add more to the architectural beauty and unity of the
> village. A Lake Street site is favored by many and among
> those suggested is the southeast corner of Lake Street and
> Kenilworth Avenue.[15]

The same story indicated that the congregation had accepted
the offer of Willis S. Herrick of Dunlop and Company for the free
use of Nakama Hall for both the regular Sunday religious services
and the Sunday school. Meetings of other church-related groups
and youth group activities would be held at the First Baptist
Church.

At the call of Mr. Skillin, the president, the board of trustees
met in a specially convened session on Sunday, June 11, and it
became quite clear that there was going to be a lot of work for
them over the next few months. The existing committee on church
and grounds was instructed to clear the church lot and get the
highest price possible for whatever they could salvage from the fire.
The board also authorized the treasurer of the parish to deposit
the funds paid as the insurance settlement, instructing him to accept
a six-month certificate of deposit for half the amount and to place
the other half in a C.D. that would mature in three months. They
then got down to the business of making appointments to the
committees as called for at the preceding Friday's meeting of the
parish. The first suggestion, by way of motion, was that "the Committee on Plans be made five in number, two being ladies," though
the minutes unfortunately failed to give any reason for the unusually specific motion. Various congregants were appointed to the
committees, each comprised of either three or five members. H.A.
Taylor was appointed to chair ways and means, J.H. Heald to chair
site, the minister to chair plans, and C.E. Roberts to chair building.

In response to the motion, two women were appointed to the committee on plans, though, curiously, none were appointed to any of the other committees.[16] It was then decided that a vacancy on any of the four committees should be filled by a majority vote of the membership of the affected committee and that the president should send the membership some sort of notice appraising them of the makeup of the committees and the nature and scope of their work.

The various committees went to work immediately, and the minister sent a letter to the board two days later, accepting the chairmanship of the plans committee. The two major committees operative were those on site and ways and means, and neither was idle. Various solicitations were made, and at a regular meeting of the Ladies Social Union, it was decided to make a pledge of $2,000 to be paid in three installments, provided the organization was not called upon to contribute any additional money to the operating expenses of the church.[17] By the time the board met on July 2, they were able to note that there was $2,916.70 in the building fund and that the old piano had been sold for $35. That amount was also committed to the fund, as was some $1,992 in insurance money to come from the loss of the building's furnishings. As it was clear that the congregation favored building elsewhere, a discussion about the value of the old church property ensued, ending in a consensus that it was worth about $7,500. Mr. Skillin and Mr. Lewis were asked to check into the matter of title preliminary to offering the property for sale.

The meeting ended with the president pointing out that though the music committee was recommending renting an organ for use in the services at Nakama Hall, it would be necessary to economize on music costs for the present. Although not even a site had been selected for a new church, music was already on the minds of people other than the music committee, and Dr. Johonnot had already received at least one solicitation from an organ company in Massachusetts, noting that "we are advised that you are about to erect a new church edifice and presume that upon its completion you will require a pipe organ for same."[18] In all, a dozen firms would eventually contact the church and inquire about plans for an organ.

The ongoing issues of the site and ways and means committees dominated the special meeting of the parish held on July 5, with Mr. Taylor, the ways and means chairman, reporting that pledges totaling $15,235 had already been either pledged or received, and that there was the possibility of additional support later. The committee was asked to continue its work.

The larger part of the meeting was devoted to a discussion about the appropriate site for the new church. Mr. Heald, the chairman of the site committee, informed the congregation that the committee had investigated several possible sites, but doubted that he could get very firm price quotes from the owners unless the parish had narrowed down their choices considerably, hopefully to one or two. Dr. Johonnot provided a statistical breakdown of the sections in which the parishioners lived, noting that about 40 percent of the parish lived east of Oak Park Avenue and 60 percent lived west; 33 percent lived north of Lake Street and 67 percent south. An informal vote indicating each member's preference for a location failed to produce more than seven votes for any one location but, as only one vote was cast for the old site, the total rejection of that location was confirmed. The votes did indicate a general disposition toward a site on or near Lake Street, and the site committee at least had their investigations focused in that area.

Yet another special meeting of the board of trustees was held on Sunday, July 7, in order to further narrow down the possible sites for the new church. After much discussion, it was decided to ask the site committee to obtain the lowest price for each of several lots in the general vicinity of Lake Street and Oak Park Avenue: the lots were the hundred feet of Mr. Cook's property facing east on Oak Park Avenue between Pleasant and Randolph Streets; the lot just east of the main post office on Lake Street and Oak Park

Avenue; the Gale lot on the corner of Lake Street and Kenilworth Avenue; "together with such other locations as the Committee may have investigated."[19]

Two other actions were taken at the same meeting. The board directed Dr. Johonnot to take his vacation at that time and also requested that the plans committee recommend an architect. No one seems to have noted the irony in that juxtaposition of motions—Dr. Johonnot being the chair of the plans committee. Though it is possible that the action was intentional, given the high regard in which the congregation held the minister, it is safe to assume that such an action was both unplanned and accidental.

A special parish meeting was held on August 1, with the sole agenda item of approving the site committee's choice of the Gale lot of 105 feet fronting on Lake Street and 150 facing Kenilworth Avenue, on the southeast corner of the two streets, providing that the property in question could be bought for no more than $10,000. There were only thirty-two members in attendance and voting, with no member of the site committee in attendance, and the vote was nineteen in favor and thirteen against the motion. Another congregational meeting was held on August 10 to formally endorse the revised purchase plan for the Gale lot, subject to the following modification: "Mr. Gale had offered 100 feet frontage by 150 feet in depth for $10,000, desiring to sell the remaining five feet of frontage to Luther Conant, whose house and lot are just adjoining on the east, Mr. Conant promising to keep the space open."[20] With a larger attendance and a clear sentiment in favor of the site, the official vote was thirty-nine favoring the purchase and only two against the motion. A move to accept the decision by acclamation was approved, and the site committee was discharged from any further duty, with the thanks of the congregation.

It should be noted and remembered that Gale was a founding member of the congregation, its first treasurer, and had made a sizable contribution toward the construction of the first church building. Clearly, he was a major player in the church and a man of influence. And, as we shall see, his sons were no less involved with the congregation and even more with the architect chosen to build the new church.

The local press was lavish in its praise for the selection of that particular site, noting:

> It is understood that this site has been the favorite of Dr. Johonnot ever since the new church has been a possibility, and it has been recognized from the start as one of the most available locations. It is directly opposite the First Congregational Church and will form one of the group of fine public buildings in the central part of the village. These two churches, on opposite sides of Lake Street, will form a good balance for the two other churches standing in like relation to each other, the First Presbyterian and the new Grace Episcopal church, directly opposite each other a little farther to the west on the same street.[21]

The same article mentioned progress toward fundraising and informed the public that about $30,000 was available for construction and concluded with what must have been viewed as merely a pious hope for the future of the yet-undesigned building but, instead, turned out to be prophetic: "Now that this site is determined upon, the question of plans will be taken up at once and the architectural design will no doubt be wholly worthy of the conspicuous place in which the edifice will stand."[22]

At the special meeting of the board of trustees called for August 13, Mr. Lewis informed the board that Nakama Hall had been rented for regular Sunday services for the following year, at a price of $25 per month, and that services would resume, as usual, in September. In addition, the group authorized the president to complete the contractual arrangements necessary for the acquisition of the Gale lot and the treasurer to make the first payment. With a site in hand and substantial commitments toward the

Figure 17. At the time Frank Lloyd Wright won the commission to build Unity Temple, he and his wife Catherine had six children and lived in the home next to his studio on the corner of Chicago and Forest Avenues. His practice was successful, but he had never had a public commission in the village.
Courtesy Frank Lloyd Wright Home and Studio

amount necessary to build a new church, the board began the serious discussion about the hiring of an architect. It was finally decided to invite the plans committee to join the trustees in a discussion of the process for the selection of an architect and the plans, at a time to be selected by President Skillin.

At the time of the fire, Frank Lloyd Wright (fig. 17) had been living in a house of his own design, a few blocks away from the new site, and had designed most of the major houses associated with the early development of the Prairie School of architecture that occupied some of the prime real estate between Chicago Avenue and the corner of Kenilworth and Lake Streets. Nearby and known by sight to all of the congregants were the so-called "bootleg" homes Wright had designed while still working for Louis Sullivan in 1892 and 1893, and such major early homes as the Winslow House of 1894 and the Chauncey Williams House of 1895 in River Forest, and the Furbeck House of 1897 and the imposing Nathan Moore House of 1895 in Oak Park. Then, in the next decade, he had completed such important Oak Park modernist Prairie homes as the Frank Thomas and the Fricke House (both 1901), the Arthur Heurtley House (1902), and the William Martin and Edwin Cheney homes (1903). The irony is that Wright had recently completed an incredible string of important homes over the past decade and was extremely active in Buffalo with the spin-off homes of the Larkin project, yet had only a couple of local projects on the drawing board at the time.

At the same time, several of his commercial buildings in Chicago and the Larkin Building in Buffalo had given him a reputation that transcended the exclusively residential work that he had designed for his Oak Park clients. Was he feeling like a prophet without honor in his own village? Given his large family and his tendency to live beyond his means, the word that a new church was to be built must have been extremely good news and caused him to work every possible contact to get the commission.

CHAPTER 2

THE ARCHITECT
AND HIS PLANS

The meeting to discuss the selection of an architect with the plans committee was held on August 30, 1905, with the board of trustees, the secretary, the treasurer, and members of the committee. The minister, as chairman of the committee, was asked to give a report on the selection process to date. He informed the board that the committee had visited quite a number of churches in the area and had spent an evening with each of nine architects discussing the needs of the church with them. He named them for the board, as follows: Mr. E.S. Hall, Mr. Williamson, Mr. E.A. Mayer, Mr. Sutcliff, Mr. Harned, Mr. Dwight H. Perkins, Mr. Frank Lloyd Wright, Mr. William A. Otis, and Mr. Patton. When the minister was "asked if the Committee could reduce the number to three or four he said that the Committee gave preference to the last four. Each one of these men was then discussed by Dr. Johonnot and the other members of the Committee enumerating points for and against each one."[1] Unfortunately, the minutes of the meeting, as taken by the secretary to the board, Dr. Guy Parke Conger, failed to mention the pros and cons of each candidate, but merely noted "the thorough and painstaking way in which the Committee had gotten the situation in hand and giving the Board of Trustees a clear insight to the situation."[2] At the end of their testimony, the committee suggested that the board have their committee work closely with the building committee.

The process for selection of an architect has only recently received attention, and was unknown to the scholars who have heretofore written about Unity Temple.[3] In large part, as it was well documented and obvious that Wright's mother had a close acquaintanceship with Augusta Chapin, who preceded Dr. Johonnot as the minister as of the congregation (and with whom the family boarded when they moved to Oak Park in 1887, as mentioned in chapter 1), it has been widely assumed and stated that Wright was not only a member of the congregation, but that, as such, had been selected as the architect.[4] However, at least the architect's primary—if not only—real church affiliation lay elsewhere, at All Souls Church on the South Side of Chicago, where he, his future wife Catherine, and her parents were listed, as early as 1886, among those "who, by their attendance or contribution, have expressed an interest in our work."[5] Mr. and Mrs. Frank L. Wright were listed at All Souls, with an Oak Park address as of 1890, and were enrolled as members from 1892 through at least 1906. As Wright's well-known Unitarian uncle, Jenkin Lloyd Jones, was the founding minister at All Souls and its guiding spirit for many years, the Wright's affiliation there is hardly surprising. Given some of the other affiliations, however, it is worth exploring the backgrounds of the other architects who had been visited by the committee, as well as to consider why they might have been rejected so quickly.

Of the five architects eliminated immediately after the first round of investigation, it is probably most surprising to note the name of Henry P. Harned (1849–1934), as he was not only the oldest and most experienced of the architects consulted, but was also a member of the Unity Church congregation at the time of the fire.[6] This is particularly important as those scholars who touted Wright's membership as a reason for his selection have always ignored the existence of Harned among the group of architects visited. Clearly, if being a member was deemed an important point in Wright's favor, the same should hold for Harned. However, as those same researchers never mention either Harned or any others under consideration, it is a reasonable assumption that they never consulted the relevant minutes of the board and accepted Wright's version of the story as the only architect under consideration. Having said that, we also have to acknowledge that Harned's reputation was as a conservative, that his work and reputation were fairly local, and that he has not lasted well. Indeed, he is hardly mentioned in any sources on area architecture of the period. Thus, given the eventual finalists and selection of an architect, it seems that the committee members who were involved in the selection were looking for something a little more adventurous than Harned was prepared to give them.

When we look a bit more closely at the list of those considered, almost as surprising was the prompt elimination of John Sutcliffe (1853–1913). Though he was not a member of the Church at all, he was a very well-known specialist in ecclesiastical architecture and an equally well-established resident of Oak Park. Sutcliffe had designed the very handsome, though thoroughly traditional, Gothic building, Grace Episcopal Church, begun in 1901 and completed only in 1905, on Lake Street, just a block west of the site of the lot purchased by the Unity Church congregation. And although his work was more conservative than the congregation probably desired, it was somewhat unusual to deny such an established local architect the opportunity to even submit a design.

William G. Williamson (1861–1922), though not an Oak Parker, had also completed a church in the suburb, the First Presbyterian Church (now Calvary Memorial Church) completed in 1902, also one block west of the proposed building, and right across the street from the Episcopal Church. Though Williamson lacked an Oak Park address, the comparative modernity of his Richardsonian building, its massive dignity, the fact that it was well received in the community, and its similarity to the church homes of other

Unitarian and liberal Universalist congregations throughout the Midwest, makes his total exclusion perplexing. We would have imagined that, based on his recent work alone, Williamson, too, would have been invited to submit a design, but that might well be our early-twenty-first-century appreciation of the Richardson Romanesque speaking, rather than a group committed to avoiding historicism of any sort.

Emory S. Hall (1869–1939) was also an architect who was active in designing various ecclesiastical and other public structures in the Chicago area, most especially Tabernacle Baptist Church and was involved in the substantial remodeling of several major theaters in downtown Chicago. Though he seems never to have done any work for the more liberal denominations, nor had any identifiable Oak Park connections, his reputation, like those of Sutcliffe and Williamson, was substantial. Of the rejected group, only E.A. Mayer is an elusive figure without a historical trail to identify him.

The reputations and the work of the three remaining finalists beside Wright, Otis, Patton, and Perkins, each deserve closer scrutiny to see what made them attractive candidates in the first place and to attempt to understand the reasons they failed to appeal to the committee—to get the nod—in the final decision.

William A. Otis (1855–1929) had studied at the École des Beaux Arts in Paris and had built a substantial professional reputation in partnership with William Le Baron Jenney, before setting out on his own. His major commissions included the first library at Northwestern University and the grand home for William French, the first director of the Art Institute of Chicago. He also built many other homes and churches, and organized the first Chicago architecture program, a partnership of the Art Institute of Chicago and the Armour Institute. Most relevant to the project at hand, however, was his design for the Hull Memorial Chapel for the First Unitarian Society that he had designed in Chicago in 1896. Much of his work looked to the colonial era or to the Italian Renaissance, though he avoided the heaviness that

Figure 18. The First Congregational Church that faces Unity Temple across Lake Street had suffered a fire and was rebuilt with the design of Normand C. Patton, an important Chicago architect who lived in Oak Park. He had also designed the Scoville Institute next to the church (far right) but didn't get the Unity Temple commission. Courtesy The Historical Society of Oak Park & River Forest

could accompany such revival work. Nonetheless, his work was certainly derivative.

The most well known of the four finalists, and probably the most successful of the entire nine, was Normand S. Patton (1852–1915). Patton had an excellent education, including training at

MIT and had established a practice in Chicago from 1874 to 1877, when he left for government work in Washington, D.C. He had returned in 1883, moving to Oak Park and doing a lot of work here and around Chicago, in the partnership of Patton and Fisher from 1885 to 1901. Patton was an extremely busy and active architect, with more than one hundred Carnegie Libraries to his credit. During his second Chicago practice era, he designed the original building for the Armour Institute (later incorporated into the Illinois Institute of Technology), the Chicago Academy of Sciences building, and buildings and plans for such other colleges at Purdue, Carleton, and Millikin. A Resident of Oak Park, he was responsible for the major rebuilding of First Congregational Church (fig. 18), designed the Scoville Institute, and was involved in the design of the high school and other civic buildings. He was a fellow of the American Institute of Architects and served as member of its board of directors for two terms. He was at the peak of his powers and influence at the time of the Unity Temple project, yet his architectural designs had as much of an historical cast as those of Otis, Williamson, and Sutcliffe. Thus, looking ahead to the conception Wright presented and to the theology espoused by both the minister and the architect, it seems possible to explain the rejection of all of their designs as too reflective of traditional church architecture.

The really difficult figure to come to grips with is Dwight Heald Perkins (1867–1941), the last of the finalists. After studies at MIT, Perkins worked briefly for H.H. Richardson before moving on to the office of Burnham and Root. Thus, he had an awareness of the latest in both building styles and technology. He had supervised the construction of the Monadnock Building in downtown Chicago and then had established his own office upon being awarded the commission for a new building by Steinway Piano Company in 1894. He shared space with Wright and others in that building and later designed several revival-style buildings for the University of Chicago before forsaking that kind of work for settlement buildings at both the University of Chicago and Northwestern University. He became the chief architect for the Chicago Board of Education in 1905 and went on to design at least forty schools, the most important being the Carl Shurz High School. Perkins was not only a Unitarian, but was also a member of All Souls Church, the church led and dominated by Wright's great uncle, Jenkin Lloyd Jones (and he also was a teacher in its Sunday school). In addition, he had many ties that made him a strong candidate for the commission, ties to the Unity Church, to All Souls Church, and even to Frank Lloyd Wright. Perkins was also related to Marion Mahony (whom we will encounter as a major figure in the story of Unity Temple). Perkins and Wright had been working together as co-architects on the ambitious Abraham Lincoln Center project for Jones through the first few years of the twentieth century, and Perkins had become the sole architect in charge in 1903. Wright himself was later to credit both his uncle and Perkins with the exterior of the Center, though he reserved the credit for the interior for himself. Given all of his experience, the modernity of his best designs, and the work he had only just completed on the Abraham Lincoln Center, it is not at all clear why he didn't get the commission, and the available records really provide us with no clues.

As stated earlier, it is debatable whether Wright was ever a member of the church or one for a very short time.[7] And even if he was, as has been pointed out in other contexts, his financial contributions and commitment to the congregation seem to have been nonexistent. There are several indications that Wright had at least some affiliation with Unity Church; his name appears on a list in a brochure that dates to 1898 and which lists all the members of the church. More recently, the congregational archivist has noted that Wright's name continues to appear on the membership lists over the next few years.[8] Part of the problem may relate to the previously mentioned church within the parish, with Wright, as a Unitarian, not part of the Universalist Church. However, as the

Figure 19. Thomas H. Gale was one of the sons of Edwin O. Gale, a realtor, and a major client of Frank Lloyd Wright's. Wright built one of the "bootleg" houses on Chicago Avenue for him and a vacation home in Michigan. Upon Gale's early death, in 1907, the architect built a home for his widow. Courtesy The Historical Society of Oak Park & River Forest

archivist points out, Wright wasn't much of an active member, to the extent he was one at all. He notes that the early document that lists pledges—with check-offs—includes Wright's name, but there is no check next to the $100 amount listed.[9]

In any case, Wright was certainly an Oak Park resident, had ties to the previous minister, Augusta Chapin, and certainly had friends and clients among members of the parish. And, perhaps, it should be among those friends and clients that we should be looking for the relationships that might have given Wright an edge over even those other well-established architects who had ecclesiastical commissions to their credit.

When we examine Wright's client base in the decade preceding the Unity Temple commission, one name jumps out, and that name is Gale. Edwin O. Gale was a founding member of the congregation, and as noted, was its first treasurer. It was also his property that the congregation purchased in order to build the new church. Not only were members of the Gale family dedicated founding members of the congregation and developers of large parts of the area (the Galewood section of Chicago just north of Oak Park is named after them), but they also were broadly involved in real estate and investments. His son Thomas H. Gale's letterhead for this point in 1905 lists his business as real estate, loans, renting, and insurance, with offices in the prestigious Tacoma Building in downtown Chicago.

Among the bootleg houses already mentioned, two of them were commissioned by sons of Edwin Gale, one for the aforementioned Thomas (fig. 19), and one for his older brother, Walter, in 1892 and 1893, respectively. In addition, Wright designed a summer home for Thomas and his wife in Michigan. The good relationship between architect and client was clearly there, as Wright was to design a new home in Oak Park for the recently widowed Mrs. (Laura) Thomas Gale in 1909 and three cottages on the Michigan property at about the same time. Having such dedicated and devoted clients among the first families of the congregation must have counted a great deal in the selection process.

But the Gales were not the only church members who had commissioned buildings by Wright or were close to him. As pointed out in Joseph Siry's monograph, the architect had built a home for George W. Smith and had designed several homes and groups of buildings for Charles E. Roberts. One set of additions and stables had been built in the 1890s, while the other designs never came to fruition, yet Wright and Roberts remained close friends. Possibly equally important is the fact that Roberts's daughter, Isabel, was Wright's office manager. She was also a client, with her Wright-designed River Forest home built while Unity Temple was under construction.

Less obvious in the maneuvering that must have taken place among the candidates, than that between friends and supporters of various architects, may have been the role of Wright's mother, Anna, who lived in the house right next door to that of her son and his family. Never very far from his side, she was always a fierce fighter on his behalf. Her probable area of support would have taken place halfway between their homes and the site of the new church. Anna Wright was a founding member of the Nineteenth Century Woman's Club (now Nineteenth Century Club), and very involved in its programs and activities. At the weekly programs, lectures, and teas, it is impossible not to imagine her having a word with the other well-connected women of the club. She would have pointed out the wonderful homes he had designed that stretched north from the club building up Forest Avenue to the corner of Chicago Avenue and the home and studio of her only son.

With the choice of an architect limited to the four mentioned finalists and a strong sense of direction provided by the board of trustees, the congregation began its new season of services on September 3. All the members had already received the minister's exhortation: "We are called to a year of strenuous work. For this I trust the vacation has made us ready. A new house for our worship and social service is to be erected. The presence and help of each member and friend of our society, young and old, will be needed."[9] The board of trustees held their regular monthly meeting later that day, at the Oak Park branch real estate office of Thomas Gale and attended to several routine matters in addition to the important business at hand, which was the construction of a new church. They first authorized the plans committee to select and hire an architect to build the church, and then requested the same body

> to cause plans and specifications to be made for the new church edifice to cost not exceeding $30,000.00 including decoration, the seating of the auditorium, and the equipment of the building for lighting and heating and excluding the organ and other furnishing and report same to the board of trustees.[10]

In order that the new building might be properly financed and to keep funds flowing in a timely fashion, the treasurer was directed to mail notices to those whose pledges to the building fund would be due on October 1. By the time the Ladies Social Union met on the 15th, James Heald Jr., the treasurer (who was the young man who had so vividly reported the destruction of the original church) had written them to ask what portion of their $2,000 pledge could be paid by the 25th. The members agreed to send $200 immediately, and as a further gesture of support, it was moved, seconded, and carried that each member would bring a dime for the building fund to every meeting.

In an often-quoted segment of *An Autobiography*, Frank Lloyd Wright informs us that he always refused to enter an architectural competition and explains why such events are blueprints for mediocrity. He then immediately states, "A competition was first thought of for Unity Temple, but the idea was abandoned and the commission was given to me after much hesitation."[11] We have already seen that the plans committee interviewed several architects and narrowed the number down to four—including the already successful Dwight Perkins and Normand S. Patton, another Oak Parker and the president of the Chicago chapter of the prestigious professional organization, the American Institute of Architects—before eventually selecting Wright. However, we find not even the suggestion that such a competition was contemplated when we examine the seemingly thorough minutes of the meetings of the various bodies involved in the selection process. Perhaps the architect misremembered or misinterpreted the perfectly normal practice of interviewing several architects as an invitation to participate in a competition, when recalling his experience almost thirty years after the fact. Either Wright's memory was faulty or he was at least oversimplifying the events surrounding one of his most important commissions. That will be apparent when we come to consider the way he seems to have conflated and compressed the events of the next few months in his telling of the story in his published autobiography. But the issue of the "competition" that never took place was very much on Wright's mind when he was writing of his involvement and the award of the commission, as he was so emphatic in his battling this particular paper tiger.

While there are no extant committee minutes to provide an exact chronology of their activities, the members of the plans committee seem to have agreed on Wright after discussing possible plans with their finalists in the next two weeks. Indeed, they may have settled on him by September 16, though it was only at a special meeting of the board of trustees, on Sunday evening, December 17, that the committee formally reported the result of their mission. They noted "that they had employed Mr. Frank L. Wright as architect, and submitted to the board plans for a new church edifice which had been prepared by Mr. Wright under the direction of the Committee and recommended the adoption and acceptance of such plans." The nature and level of detail of those plans would be fascinating to study, but we don't have any hard documentation as to what was shown to the committee at first. As a religious philosophy and thoughts about what the building should not be had already been under discussion before the fire, it is entirely possible that Wright concentrated on the issues of form and its relationship to doctrinal issues. So, it is appropriate that we start by examining what Wright had to say about those issues, both to the committee and to posterity.

In the widely read, revised 1943 edition of *An Autobiography*, Wright devotes about seven pages to recount his idea for the church, the development of his plan, and how he sold it all to the building committee; but his version of the story is so much at variance with the minutes and records of the church that the story bears careful examination. Aside from the facts surrounding the chronology and the personnel involved in the commission, which we will discuss at length, Wright's story of how and why he developed his plan is valuable not only for the description of his creative process, but also for what it tells us about the way he could develop a philosophical rationale to justify the design.

He begins the chapter by describing the pastor's traditional and conventional expectations, and by implication, the expectations of the congregation as a whole:

> [H]ad Doctor Johonnot, the Universalist pastor of Unity
> Church, been Fra Junipero the style of Unity Temple
> would have been predetermined—"Mission." Had he been
> Father Latour it would have been Midi-Romanesque. Yes,
> and perhaps being what he was, he was entitled to the only
> tradition he knew—that of the little white New England
> church, lean spire pointing to heaven—"back East." If sen-
> timentality were sense this might be so.
>
> But the pastor was out of luck. Circumstances brought
> him to yield himself up in the cause of architecture.[12]

Having challenged the committee to reject the a priori aesthetics of tradition, he recounts a story, a story that explains God's
interest in man's involvement in mankind, to soften them up for the
type of radically different design he had in mind for the new
church.

> Did they not know the tale of the holy man who, yearn-
> ing to see God, climbed up and up the highest mountain—
> climbed to the highest relic of a tree there was on the
> mountain? There, ragged and worn, he lifted up his eager
> perspiring face to heaven and called upon God. He heard
> a voice bidding him get down…go back!
>
> Would he really see God's face? Then he should go back,
> go down there in the valley below where his people were—
> there only could he look upon God's countenance.[13]

With the issue of God's interest in man contrasted to the conventional steeple pointing to the heavens, the architect continued
his story and proposed a temple to man, a place where man would
study man as per the desire of God—"[a] modern meeting house
and a good-time place." And what was Wright proposing but the
description and even the name of the New England meeting house,
but without the architectural style usually associated with the image

of the meeting house. He hoped to interest the pastor, personally, through his parable, and he informs us that he succeeded: "The pastor was a liberal. His liberality was thus challenged, his reason was piqued and the curiosity of all was aroused."[14] Having aroused their curiosity, and with them asking what such a meeting house might look like, Wright, with the instinct of a born showman, gave them not an inkling of his plans. He told them, "'That's what you came to me for....I can imagine it and I will help you create it.' Promising the building committee something tangible to look at soon—I sent them away."[15] The implication is clearly to be taken that, at that time, the architect had nothing in mind but the idea of replacing the New England church with something different, something innovative and modern.

Whether the initial plan, the design in brick that Sidney Robinson so clearly describes in the foreword, was ever seen by the committee is debatable, and it is entirely possible that they never saw that version. As the extant model of the building would seem to predate the December meeting at which the plan was accepted, and that model was already in a later form of the design and in concrete, it seems probable that the working out of the first stages of the design took place exclusively in the mind and on the paper of the architect in his studio. Yet it is also tempting to speculate on whether he showed Roberts or another ally his direction and tested out his ideas, and there is some evidence to suggest that such was the case. The model of the building is that evidence, as we shall see.

We have already noted that the plans committee was comprised of five individuals: Dr. Johonnot (chairman), Mrs. Bryant, Edwin H. Ehrman, Mr. Jackson, and Mrs. Lewis. The building committee was comprised of Charles Roberts (chairman), Frank Adams, and Henry P. Harned, and that the two had agreed to work together after August 30. Whether they were doing so or not is hard to know, but, if so, there would have been a total of those eight. Yet, in the course of a few pages, Wright speaks of the building committee as "all good men and true,"[16] when recounting how

the majority of the committee members were won over after seeing his plans and model. He also mentions the number of committee members as seven, and names the one remaining negative
voice as that of Mr. Skillin.[17] It is also quite surprising that Wright
makes no mention of the fact that Harned was the same man who
was an architect candidate for the commission. Although it is possible that Wright didn't know that Harned had been considered
and rejected, it is interesting that he makes no reference to having
an architect on the working committee at all.

It is very difficult both to sort out the group or groups Wright
was talking to and over what period of time the conversations
took place, due to the incongruities in the above-mentioned
account. Only if the architect were talking exclusively to the
building committee rather than the combined building and plans
committees would or could he be referring to them as "good men
and true," for two members of the plans committee were women.
Yet, were he addressing only the former, the number of members
was three, not seven. And while we can perhaps assume that the
number seven itself came about as the result of a resignation or
ongoing absence, it does not seem possible to concede the term
"good men and true" as either mere poetic license or as sarcasm
in this context. The other really incongruous and inexplicable fac-
tor is the naming of Mr. Skillin as one of the group. Skillin was still
the president of the board of trustees as of the date of the events
under discussion and had appointed the members of all the
committees—but was a member of neither of them. One line of
response accounts for both the presence of Skillin and the lack of
women among the committee: we should assume that he was talking about subsequent meetings with the board of trustees rather
than the building and plans committees. The board of trustees consisted of six men, plus a secretary and a treasurer who were also
both men. As attendance was often imperfect, and the minutes
show the treasurer most likely to be absent if his presence was not
essential, it is entirely possible that the apparent membership of a

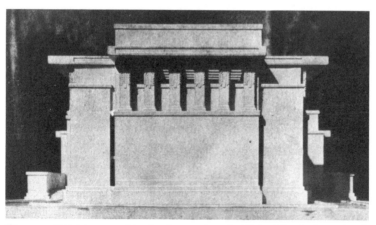

Figure 20. Wright was working hard to convince the Unity Church "committee" of the soundness of his radical design for their new building when his ally, C.E. Roberts, suggested that he build a model to explain the structure and its design.

committee of the whole of the board could have been seen by Wright as consisting of seven men.

Unfortunately, while addressing one set of problems of identity, such a solution would create another. Wright recounts the battle to convince the "committee" with particular relish: "All right; let the committee come now. They do come—all curious. Soon confounded—taking the 'show me' attitude."[18] He then goes on to explain how he wins them over, with his ally, Roberts, after the inventor urged him to build a model to illustrate his points (fig. 20). The model was built of plaster, and it shows the major configuration of the building and the massings, without much detail. And, though we will see that there were many changes made during construction, the basic form and feel of the building is much the way it appeared in the model.

Again, with respect to the model, it seems reasonable to assume that Roberts had seen the results of the evolution of the plan from longitudinal and brick to Greek Cross and concrete, from the first drawings that Wright had developed, until he arrived at the structure as finally built. There were other changes as well: the changes to the inner staircases, the access to the lower floor, the housing around the colored glass, and the arrangement of the glass in the ceiling being the most important. Changes in lighting, both in terms of placement and appearance were also important. In the foreword, Robinson describes how the brick concept was to work and how the structure was to work as the traditional "post and beam," and then leads us through the subsequent design and the working drawings that—for the most part—reflect the reality of the building today. Yet, again, we have to both note that changes were made during construction, and that there would have been others if Ehrman and the congregational leadership had not stood firm in rejecting many of them.

Recognizing the unusual nature of the design and materials, Roberts must have been aware of their potential for controversy, and he pushed for the model. In this sense, Roberts might have been the great collaborator, whether an official member of the selection committee or not. And, if so, it helps explain the credit Wright always gave to him. The model seems to have done the trick, and proved to at least some of the skeptics that the project could work. Wright's prose is as purple as any his esteemed teacher, Sullivan, ever penned, but he does provide a fascinating blow by blow:

> We use all our resources, we two—the inventor and I—and we win a third member of the committee at the first meeting. Including the pastor, there are now only four left in doubt. One of the four openly hostile—Mr. Skillin. Dr. Johonnot, the pastor, is himself impressed but cautious—oh very—but tactful. He really has a glimpse of a new world. There is hope, distinctly hope, when he makes four as he soon does and the balance of power is with us. We need three more but the architect's work is done now. The four will get the others. The pastor is convinced. He will work![19]

The problem with identifying this group as being the board of trustees, of course, is that neither the minister nor Charles Roberts were members of that board. Even if we hypothesize that they met with the board as the heads of the two committees in a one-step process, we once again would find a discrepancy in numbers, creating the need for eight votes, not seven. There seems to be no way to accept the architect's account of the process, and we must return to the church's records to review the process as seen through board minutes and related documents.

According to the minutes of the board of trustees meeting of December 17, as described above, and after the plans had been explained by the committee and considered by the board, the meeting adjourned until the coming Tuesday evening.[20] At that adjourned special meeting, held on the 19th, the subject was not the selection of the architect and his plans, but rather the matter of raising sufficient funds to pay for a new church. The members of the ad hoc ways and means committee were in attendance and reviewed their success in soliciting subscriptions to date. They then joined the board in a discussion about the probable amount that could be raised for this purpose. They came to no conclusion, however, and agreed to meet again, at the call of the president. The next special meeting was held on January 2, 1906, to consider and discuss the reports of both the plans and finance committees, though without the members of those committees being present. Mr. Skillin announced that the congregation had finally been able to sell the old church property to a Mr. Rogers for $6,500, and that those monies were now able to be included in the calculation of funds available for the proposed new church. With the sale of the lot, the insurance settlement, the cash in hand, and the pledges, "it was estimated that the cost of the new church complete (taking the figures of the one contractor who has submitted estimates) would exceed by $8,000 to $10,000 the present resources of the Society." In spite of the inadequacy of available funds, there was strong sentiment in favor of moving ahead, and "the general opinion was that amount should not stand in the way if it will get what we want."[21]

The discussion then turned to the plans themselves, as submitted by Wright and recommended by the plans committee. The various board members had questions about a wide variety of issues relating to the design, the space available for certain functions, the seating capacity of the auditorium, lighting, and ventilation. They were also concerned with the suggestion that concrete construction be used, questioning whether it could do the job required of it. This being the first time the plans were being discussed since they had been presented by the committee, and with all of the above questions in mind, "Mr. Lewis moved to adjourn to meet at Mr. Frank Lloyd Wright's Thursday at 8 P.M." The meeting took place as scheduled, with the minutes indicating that the entire board, the treasurer, and the secretary were present; there was no indication that there were any guests. "The plans for the new church were carefully examined, the members of the Board asking questions and Mr. Wright explaining. After the Board had exhausted its list of questions and objections to details thought to be weak the meeting adjourned informally about 10 P.M."[22]

The next three months were filled with many meetings, both in regard to the actual plans for the building and also in regard to the congregation's ability to pay for the entire project upon completion. The minutes of the board meetings are usually devoted to either one of those issues or the other, though occasionally they took up both. Depending upon whether the board was meeting alone or with one or both of the other committees, the composition and number of attendees changes, but at no one time does it approximate the group of seven as described by the architect. At the same time the architect was responding to some of the concerns that had been developed by a newly formed joint committee, and working the design up into final plans, specifications, and detailed drawings: he was also concurrently involved with the bidding process.

One of the most crucial of the many "special" meetings was a special joint meeting of the board of trustees with both the plans and the building committees, held at the home of President Skillin on Sunday evening, January 14, 1906. Five of the six trustees, four of the five members of the plans committee, and two of the three members of the building committee attended, as did the treasurer and the secretary of the parish. The president reviewed the financial picture in regard to the funds available for the construction of a new church, "In pledges to the new church fund $22,000, Insurance $9,500, Old lot $6,500, $1,000 in Building Fund giving a total in assets of $39,000. The new lot cost $11,000, leaving $28,000 in pledges and cash in hand." It was suggested that another $2,000 might be raised through pledges from those who had yet to make a commitment and that an additional $2,000 to $3,000 might be given by those congregants who had already made pledges. With the plans committee estimating the cost of the building at some $40,000, a debt of $9,000 (plus $2,500 for debt service related to deferred pledge income), loomed ahead for up to a five-year period. This fiscal reality was the basis for a discussion of three possible plans of action; whether to go ahead with the building as planned, borrowing money to pay for the completed building; whether to make radical adjustments to the proposal as designed, to cut down the costs; or, whether, as Mr. Skillin proposed, to build the Unity House first, using it as an all-purpose building until there were sufficient funds in hand to build the auditorium. The reasons advanced for a two-tiered building program, with Unity House being constructed first, were stated as follows:

> Freedom from debt. Saving by not incurring running expenses. Saving by not having interest to pay. Gain by having money not yet needed at interest. Having less at stake in part than in all the building, if concrete construction is at all experimental. Some points of the Auditorium being in dispute it would give ample time in which to settle all

such, particularly as the building practicably cannot be altered after it is built. All building being very expensive at present it was hoped that in a couple of years it might be less. An additional room wanted by the ladies might be afforded under this scheme. The psychological thought that people would see that we were working to complete the church edifice and would work and give to accomplish it, and that it is difficult to make them pay for a thing already in use. That new people would be more likely to come to us if not in debt.[23]

Other board members were equally as interested in going ahead with the entire package, and they used the reverse of most of the arguments in support of the entire construction process. On the financial side, it was argued that,

should building expenses be any less in a few years, money would also be scarce, pledges hard to get and to collect. That more interest and enthusiasm could be developed with a beautiful new and *complete* church home in view than if its completion were put off two or three years. That some people might be willing to pay only part of their pledges now if Unity House was built first.... That if a separate bid was obtained for Unity House one could not know what its proportionate cost should be, hence the possibility of our unknowingly paying more than its worth, and the total of the two (Unity House and Auditorium built separately) costing considerably more.

Somewhat more surprising was the unidentified opinion that suggested that a debt of $10,000 was a "small thing" on a project of $51,000 (including the land). For, considering the difficulty previously encountered in attracting support for a new building, a debt of one-quarter to one-third of the projected construction cost was certainly a large and understandably serious concern to members of the board of trustees. And though no one was making a major case of their concerns and doubts about the materials or forms of construction when it came to actually voting on the proposal, clearly Mr. Skillin had already expressed grave reservations and had used the financial issue to launch his attack on the project. While Wright seems to have confused the makeup of the various committees, as discussed above, and we don't know just where in the process he and Mr. Skillin came into open disagreement, he certainly remembered Mr. Skillin's reactions, quite clearly, when recounting the matter some thirty years after the fact. "Doubts and fears are finally put to sleep—all but Mr. Skillin's," Wright wrote. "Mr. Skillin is sure the room will be dark—sure the acoustics will be bad....Usually there is a Mr. Skillin on every modern building project in Usonia."[24]

Most of the members of the board of trustees approved of and supported the architect's plans and ideas, so they countered the arguments about labor costs and the untested use of concrete as a building material, as specifically as they had rejected those criticisms based on financial grounds. They noted:

> That this sort of construction requires but little skilled and organized labor and that building expenses may increase instead of diminish in the next few years. That if concrete was experimental for the entire edifice it certainly was the same thing for Unity House, hence if it was considered for Unity House then in reality it was believed in whether admittedly or not, and that the two sections of the building could not be made to match if built in different times.

A middle ground was advocated by some board members who wished to see the entire structure built at one time but who were, nonetheless, concerned about finances. They suggested that the two parts of the building be completed together, but with the omission of the organ, the pews in the Auditorium, and perhaps even delaying the painting of interior surfaces, until they were in the position of being able to afford to complete those items. A final decision on how to proceed was postponed, and the minutes of the meeting noted that "it was generally understood that the general scheme of the plans drawn by Mr. Wright and recommended by the Plans committee was satisfactory.... On motion the meeting adjourned to meet at the home of Mr. Lewis (for continued discussion) Thursday January 18 at 8 P.M."[25]

The adjourned special meeting of the board met, as scheduled, with members of the plans, building, and finance committees in attendance; Frank Lloyd Wright was also there, by invitation. The minutes note that Paul Mueller had been expected but was delayed in New Orleans. Mueller had been the foreman for Adler and Sullivan when Wright first joined that firm in 1887, and had since gone out on his own as a major Chicago contractor, taking on multiple major projects and subcontracting out the various components of each project. There is no prior mention of his name in the documents relating to Unity Temple before this meeting on the 18th, but given the discussions that evening, we can see that the figures under discussion by the board for the past several meetings had been supplied for Wright by Mueller. Before turning their attention to financial matters, however, Wright went over some of the remaining technical questions with those present, particularly in regard to the perceived problems of moisture and the radiation of heat in regard to concrete construction, questions that would turn out to be prophetic. In response to the question of possibly sequencing the construction of the parts of the building, as previously mentioned, Wright estimated the cost of limiting the current project to a completed Unity House, based on figures obtained from Paul Mueller's office, at $18,294. He then proceeded to advocate building the entire structure as a unit, working on the issue of price:

[He] offered to guarantee that the entire edifice, present plans unaltered, would be completed for $35,000, including architect's fee, seating of Auditorium, tinting walls, movable screens, walks, grading, planting shrubbery everything complete. He thought $2,800 might be saved for the present by omitting the seating of the Auditorium, tinting and finishing but promised to obtain more exact figures showing the cost of Unity House complete and the Auditorium complete on the exterior only.[26]

The once-again-adjourned special meeting of the board of trustees was held on the next Sunday, at noon, right after services, with three members of the finance committee in attendance as fund-raising for the new church was once again the primary agenda item. Mr. Taylor, the chairman of the ways and means committee (interchangeably referred to as the finance committee), informed those present that the building fund contained pledges in the sum of $17,500, at the moment, but added that he thought additional pledges could be secured.[27] John Lewis, one of the members of the board, seems to have taken a serious leadership role, beginning with this meeting. He moved that the finance committee prepare a special list of any parish members who had yet to subscribe or pledge to the building fund and, at a subsequent meeting, present the names of those individuals to the board so each board member could contact specific individuals about pledges. The motion was adopted. Mr. Lewis also resurfaced the issue of having the church built in stages or all at once and became the spokesman for the second option. He advocated building both parts of the plan, the Auditorium and Unity House right away, leaving the interior details to a later date, if necessary. He further suggested that Wright's plans be accepted with the understanding that people would be approached for additional donations as it is made clear just how much is needed.[28]

With all the financial matters either resolved or a plan of action for each accepted, President Skillin then brought up an important structural matter. He "declared that the main floor of the Auditorium was not large enough in the present plan and said that Mr. Wright had told him the distance between the columns could be increased."[29] The board of trustees agreed with their president and, during the same meeting, asked Mr. Skillin and the minister to take the matter up with the architect and to have such a change made in the plans for the Auditorium. This change, we shall see as we study the evolution of the plans, was indeed made almost immediately. The agreement that the board members would approach individuals about special subscriptions to the building fund was honored at the next regular meeting, on February 4, when the sole agenda item was the distribution of the names to be contacted.

The board returned to the momentous issue of Wright's plans for a new church at a continuation of their regular meeting held on February 7, in the company of the minister and the architect. A letter sent by Edwin O. Gale in reference to the proposed plans was read, and though the minutes don't reveal the contents thereof, it is reasonable to assume that he had objections to some aspect of the conception. Various objections to some parts of the plan, held by present board members were discussed, and Wright also presented an alternative plan for seating in the Auditorium (fig. 21). John Lewis, who had already shown himself to be a strong advocate for the Wright design, and whose wife had been a member of the plans committee, once again took control of the direction of the meeting by moving to get the plans approved both in principle and in the general scheme of design and materials. He made a motion that covered the range of issues before the board with the following:

> Resolved that the plans for the new church prepared by
> Mr. Frank Lloyd Wright, architect, and recommended by
> the Plans Committee, be and the same hereby are approved

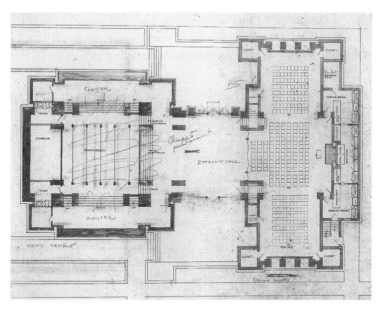

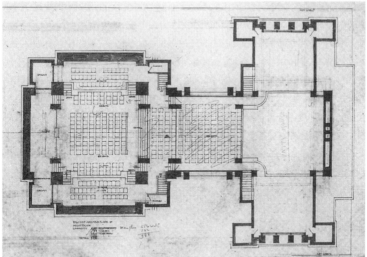

Figure 21. The original and short-lived plan for the auditorium indicated a longitudinal church with seating all the way down the center. Later drawings show the seating on three sides, and with the staircases on all sides, the way it was finally constructed.

and adopted, so far as their general plan and scheme and mode of construction are concerned, with the understanding and on the condition that the plans can be executed, including all the particulars specified in the resolution of this Board passed on the 3rd day of September 1905, and including architect's fees, for not exceeding Thirty-six Thousand Two-Hundred Dollars ($36,200.00).[30]

Having moved the board off center on the broader issue, through the unanimous adoption of that resolution, Mr. Lewis then moved another multifaceted resolution designed to establish a procedure for getting both the remaining design issues resolved and the plans into the form of actual working drawings, as follows:

Resolved, that the plans for the new church recommended to this Board by the Plans Committee be referred to a special committee consisting of the Plans Committee, the Building Committee and the Trustees, and that said Committee cause to be prepared detailed drawings and specifications in proper form for obtaining bids, and that said Committee be given full authority to make such alterations in the plans submitted as it may deem best and to finally determine all details and arrangements relating to the plans and the mode of construction of the building. Said Committee is instructed to procure bids for the erection of the building complete with the exception of the interior finishing of the Auditorium, and to report such plans, specifications and bids to this Board.[31]

That the board was finally committed to the construction of the church basically as approved by the plans committee, several months earlier, was as much a source of relief to Wright and his studio as it was to the congregation's leadership. Charles White, a Wright apprentice during the period in which Unity Temple was designed, commented on the difficulties involved in getting to the point of agreement in a letter to a friend written on March 4, "The chief thing at Wright's is of course Unity Church, the sketches of which are at last accepted, after endless fighting. We have all pleaded and argued with the committee, until we are well nigh worn out."[32] He also noted, "All hands are working on the working drawings. The building will cost about thirty-five thousand."[33]

The *Oak Leaves* edition of Saturday, February 24, gave front-page attention to the recently approved design under the heading "Unity Plans Unique," with so strong a claim for the originality of the building that one suspects that Wright himself was responsible for the story:

> The new Unity Church building, plans for which have just been completed by Frank Lloyd Wright, and half-tones of which are given in this issue of Oak Leaves, will be the most radical departure from traditional church architecture ever attempted. The whole structure, foundation, walls, floor and roof, will be of cement, reinforced where neces-sary by steel, fireproof and eternal as the hills.[34]

Although the story in the local press, White's comments, and the minutes of the previous board meeting indicate that Wright's design had been accepted before March 4, it is equally clear that the unusual design and choice of materials was still seen as prob-lematic, and it was decided to educate the congregation and win their support for the yet-unbuilt structure. John Lewis continued in his role of chief and most active supporter. At the regularly scheduled board meeting held that evening, he rose and proposed that a group of three: Frank Lloyd Wright, the architect; Dr. Johon-not, the minister; and Charles S. Woodard, a member of the con-gregation, be asked to write and prepare a booklet that would explain both the design and the rationale for the design to parish members and other interested parties. The motion carried, the three men were subsequently appointed, and the brochure, *The New Edifice of Unity Church*, appeared some three months later.[35]

It is very interesting that Wright never mentions Lewis, in the same way that he never mentions others in his *Autobiography*, though Lewis played a major role in the Unity Temple story. Instead, he concentrates on emphasizing Roberts, to the exclusion of all others but the minister. That is not to say that Roberts wasn't a supporter, nor of no influence, but we have just seen that there is clear documentary evidence of Lewis's support and commitment to the entire project, yet he is totally absent from the narrative.

March 4 was a historic date in the story of Unity Temple, marking the end of a brief but turbulent period. Not only was the decision made to publish the brochure that marks the ultimate commitment to go ahead with the plan, but there are three major personnel changes as well. Frank Adams resigned his position on the building committee, and his resignation was accepted at that meeting. Of far greater importance, it was Thomas Skillin's last meeting as both president and as a member of the board of trustees, as he did not stand for reelection. But, ultimately of the most importance and far more fateful, was the decision of the nominating committee to nominate Edwin H. Ehrman (a major business partner of Charles Roberts) as a new member of the board of trustees.

CHAPTER 3

UNITY TEMPLE: DESIGN AND JUSTIFICATION

From the start, the architect had challenged the minister and the members of the "committee" to reject the traditional New England church with its spire in favor of "a temple to man, appropriate to his uses as a meeting-place, in which to study man himself for his God's sake."[1] And though, as discussed, the board of trustees had finally decided to go along with the experiment in both design and materials, and the local press had so favorably reported on the proposal, the decision to publish a brochure explaining it to the membership indicates at least their recognition of how unusual and unconventional was the project to which they were committing. Perhaps, considering the Christmas appeal letter of 1904, with its statement that the perfectly traditional Gothic Revival church then in use did not represent current ideas of church architecture, the proposed brochure was meant to explain and justify the current ideology within the Universalist movement to a wider audience than the Unitarian and more conservative congregants of Unity Church. Certainly Dr. Johonnot, an educated and deeply thoughtful member of the Universalists, was aware of those ideas, even if peers of a more radical persuasion than his own promulgated them. And, conservative is a very relative term, with the Unitarians themselves considered beyond the pale by more traditional and mainstream Trinitarian Protestants.

After examining the rhetoric that both Wright and the minister were to use in laying the groundwork for acceptance of the design of the new church building, we shall return to the issue of Universalist ideology and evaluate its possible impact on that design.

In *An Autobiography*, Wright tells us a great deal about both his idea as to how the building should function and look, and about the way he conceived of bringing those ideas to fruition through his design. First, he dealt with what he accepted and presented as the philosophical framework for the sanctuary, the auditorium: "The first idea was to keep a noble room for worship in mind, and let that sense of the great room shape the whole edifice. Let the room inside be the architecture outside."[2] But, as Sidney Robinson has pointed out so cogently, "suggesting that the design began with the interior bestows a significance that the chronology of changes does not support." He further notes that Wright claimed to be bringing the outside of the building inside, but raises the legitimate question of which came first. If, as stated above, the starting point was the "great room," would he not—in fact—want to be making the shape of the interior space overt in the appearance of the building from the outside? Robinson's conclusion is that Wright's need to see and present the outside and inside as a seamless entity is part of the architect's romantic nature, and his later wish to see unity in the parts of the building is justified, and the fact that we can plainly see the difference between outside and inside doesn't take anything away from the majesty and significance of the building.

After talking about the other needs of the congregation, especially recognizing the necessity for housing secular and educational activities, Wright thought about ways to avoid an impact on the room for prayer:

[B]ut there was a secular side to Universalist church activities—entertainment often, Sunday school, feasts, and so on. To embody these with the temple would spoil the simplicity of the room—the noble Room in the service of man for the worship of God. So I finally put the secular space designated as "Unity House," a long free space to the rear of the lot, as a separate building to be subdivided by movable screens for Sunday school or on occasion. It thus became a separate building but harmonious with the Temple—the entrance to both to be the connecting link between them. That was that."[3]

The departure from the expected norm and the change in both the exterior and interior appearance of the projected building was immediately defended by Dr. Johonnot, in a statement quoted in the same newspaper article that had first announced and illustrated the design, in February. Clearly, he is starting with Wright's premise about the need for an appropriate style to reflect the church's interests and needs, but it is equally clear that he has been convinced of the value of the design and is expressing his support in his own old-fashioned but convincing rhetorical style:

Two reasons in the main have determined the style of architecture of Unity Church: First, the desire to make the building expressive of the faith held by the worshipers; second, the necessity imposed by local conditions of creating a building with a distinct character of its own.

A recent writer on church architecture has raised the question whether a church building ought not to set forth by its form the character of the faith it represents. So far as possible this seems desirable.[4]

The minister then goes on to quote the architectural writer and critic, Charles DeKay, with an analogy picturesque enough even for Wright, "Perhaps we are on the threshold of a new era in ecclesiastical architecture when one congregation will not copy another as one man copies another man's coat, but the architect will be asked to say something to the point which cannot be misunderstood by believers." He then concludes his defense in terms of DeKay's (and Wright's) position:

> It is in this spirit that Unity Church has been designed. It is fitting that Unity Church, which represents a faith based upon reason and not upon tradition nor precedent, should depart from traditional forms of architecture. Refusing to be bound by mere precedent in theology, it may properly depart from the conventional form of architecture, if there is good reason for so doing. True originality in architecture is as desirable and inspiring as in other forms of art, if its basis is rational and the result is beautiful.... While departing widely from the traditional forms of a church architecture, the building is distinctly religious and reverential in feeling and spirit. From the broad viewpoint characteristic of the liberal interpretation of Christianity for which Unity Church stands the vital question about a church edifice is not, Does it look like other churches? But rather, Does it have the qualities of stability, dignity and reverence that make for nobility. These qualities this building possesses in a marked degree. It impresses the beholder with a sense of dignity and permanence befitting a house of worship and it has a chaste, simple spirit of beauty uplifting to the emotions. Informed with the spirit which characterized the ancient temples, it thus becomes associated with that spirit of worship which has caused man in all ages to rear temples unto God.[5]

Having warmed up with such high-flown rhetoric, Dr. Johonnot was ready and able to work on the brochure that was meant to explain the new structure, yet unbuilt, to his congregation.

Aside from its unconventional appearance, though having roots in both ancient and early American architecture, it was the choice of materials, and particularly concrete construction, that frightened some of the members of the board and made all of them sensitive to the need to have a detailed understanding of the design proposal. In spite of Wright's recollection of the "committee's concern with style" and his belief that "at this moment the creative architect is distinctly at a disadvantage as compared with his obsequious brother of the 'styles,' he who can show his pattern-book, speak glibly of St. Mark's at Venice or Capella Palatine, impress the no less craven clients by brave show of erudite authorities," it was the technical and structural elements that most concerned President Skillin and other board members.[6] Indeed, on the same page of his recollections, Wright states, "Mr. Skillin is sure the room will be dark—sure the acoustics will be bad." And, as we learned through the debates on whether to build both parts or Unity House first, Mr. Skillin and others had questioned the experimental nature of concrete construction.

The evolution of the design of Unity Temple, per se, is explored thoroughly by Robinson, but it is important to remember that Wright had not originally conceived of the building as being composed of that material but, rather, of brick. As we have already confronted the difficulty of tracing the acceptance of the design by the building committee and, subsequently, the board of trustees, we can not be sure which members of the congregation ever saw the drawings of the building in brick, and what they might have thought of the change to concrete. The negative comments quoted above only refer to the experimental nature of concrete construction, and the discussions of the board of trustees, as recorded in their minutes, never mention brick at all, so it is possible that brick construction was never a realistic option by the time the plans were brought before the members of the board.[7] Further, we have no idea as to whether or not they were aware of the architect's use of concrete as the structural core of the E-Z Polish factory, under construction in Chicago, since the past September. In any case, it is safe to assume that Wright had switched to concrete for the sake of trying to stay within the budget for the building, especially when, by using concrete, he could reuse the wooden forms for each of the major sections. We cannot point to any documents to explain material changes but Wright's admission in his *Autobiography* that "concrete was cheap."[8]

Of course, Wright was just seeing the final touches put on the E-Z Polish factory in Chicago, at the time that he was starting to think about Unity Temple, and that factory had been Wright's first use of concrete as a major element of construction. Not only that, but it is reasonably certain that he planned to have Paul Mueller, the man who had served as the builder on the E-Z project, the Larkin Building in Buffalo, and other projects, work with him again, and Mueller had the advantage of knowing what had to be done.

Some of the disquietude of the board of trustees was reflected in the minutes of a special meeting held on April 28, 1906, soon after the newly elected board had chosen its officers. There, Mr. Lewis felt the need to have the board readopt the resolution accepting the plans and specifications prepared by the architect and one that mandated the construction of both parts of the building. Even the minister, so eloquent in his defense of the plans, was concerned enough to have written a letter read by the new president, W.G. Adams, in which he suggested that a congregational meeting be called to approve going ahead with construction of the entire project. Mr. Lewis's viewpoint prevailed, however, and it was agreed to "place Dr. Johonnot's letter on file."[9] Again, it is Lewis who keeps pushing for acceptance of Wright's unaltered plans and with no justification needed to move ahead. We might well wonder if Dr. Johonnot was being sensitive to the concerns of the major new officers, but he might also have been increasingly concerned himself about the issue of cost.

With the new board committed in its support of the plans for the new church, the minister seems to have thrown himself into the work on the brochure, which appeared about six weeks later as *The New Edifice of Unity Church* (fig. 22), published by "The New

Unity Church Club."[10] In spite of a major Wright biographer's allegation that it was "a pamphlet purportedly written by Dr. Johonnot but with Wright's hand plainly visible behind the doctor's hand," and with the recognition that the minister had obviously been influenced by the architect's rhetoric and passionate justification of his design, a comparison of the prose with both the minister's statement quoted above and his various written communications to the congregation seem to point to his direct authorship.[11] Also, given Dr. Johonnot's status and learning, it is very hard to imagine him allowing himself to be merely the vehicle for Wright's words; he was both too principled and self-confident a man for that to have happened.

The brochure is really an extraordinary document, utilizing a variety of typefaces, carefully printed, and incorporating seven drawings and plans for the building, including Marion Mahony's early drawing of the west façade as a double-paged centerfold. The brochure was written, printed, and distributed in just a few weeks. Clearly, it was meant to serve several purposes: to explain this unusual and unconventional building to the members of the congregation, allaying their fears and appealing both to their liberalism and their receptivity to innovation; to aid in drawing the strongest possible financial support from that congregation; to defend the unusual appearance of the prominently placed structure to the entire community, continuing the process started by the minister in the article in the above-quoted *Oak Leaves* article in February. It is all the more remarkable that such a project was undertaken when we consider that this was a document written to support the position and to justify the beliefs of a congregation of just 125 families in a small suburb of Chicago, rather than the denominational headquarters in a major metropolis.

The New Edifice of Unity Church brochure begins with an extremely self-conscious preamble, explaining the reason for being written and informing the reader of the innovative design of the new church building:

Every radical departure from the customary must make its appeal to reason to determine its worth and truth. Without good reason we should not depart from the customary. Especially is this true in regard to things sacred. But if the change is governed by sound reason, it compels an adjustment of thought.

Figure 22. The New Edifice of Unity Church *booklet was designed by a committee of three—Dr. Johonnot, Wright, and Charles S. Woodard—and printed by a Chicago press owned by a member of the congregation.*

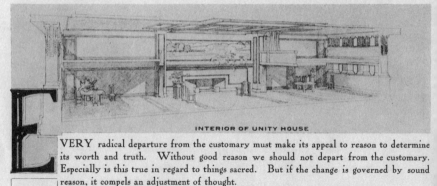

INTERIOR OF UNITY HOUSE

EVERY radical departure from the customary must make its appeal to reason to determine its worth and truth. Without good reason we should not depart from the customary. Especially is this true in regard to things sacred. But if the change is governed by sound reason, it compels an adjustment of thought.

In the new edifice designed for Unity Church by Frank Lloyd Wright, so striking an innovation has been made in church architecture as to make desirable a public description of the design and a statement of the reasons for its adoption, in order that its meaning and *raison d'etre* may be more fully understood.

DESCRIPTION

IN GENERAL

The fundamental principle of all architecture is that the form must fit the function; that is, a building must be adapted to the uses to which it is to be put and should express those uses in its form. A modern church building has a two-fold purpose; it is erected for the worship of God and for the service of man. These two functions demand a different

In the new edifice designed for Unity Church by
Frank Lloyd Wright, so striking an innovation has been
made in church architecture as to make desirable a public
description of the design and a statement of the reasons for
its adoption, in order that its meaning and *raison d'etre* may
be more fully understood.[12]

*It was commissioned and paid for by an ad hoc group, the New Unity Church
Club, in June 1906.*
Courtesy Unity Temple Restoration Foundation

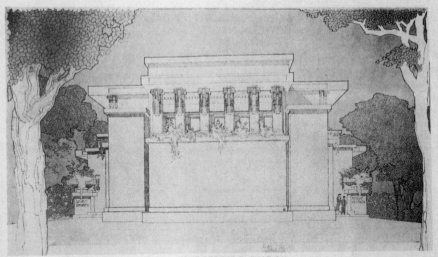

LAKE STREET ELEVATION

The choir is placed on the side next to the Entrance Hall in an alcove similar to those at the rear
and sides of the nave, and on a level with them. These four alcoves form the arms of a Greek cross.
The organ is directly behind the choir, but on a higher level, while the pulpit-platform is in front of the
choir and separated from it by a high rail and at a lower level, projecting into the nave. Behind the
organ are rooms for the choir, trustees and pastor's study, which are reached from the choir-alcove.
They form the second story of the Entrance Hall. A gallery is carried around the three sides of the

The first major heading of the text is titled "Description" and is divided into two unequal parts. The first, "In General," expands on Wright's passage defining the two major activities of the congregation, the worship service and the social, justifying their separation in the two major components of the structure. This section also contains an explanation for the nomenclature of the building parts, with particular reference to biblical justification for the use of the term Temple, though that particular rhetoric was really unrelated to the architect's design concerns. The second part, "In Detail," is the largest section in the brochure, and it provides information on the form of concrete construction, its placement on the site, and gives a fairly complete analysis of the spaces, structure, and detailing, all with specific measurements.

The second of the three sections, "The Conditions Determining the Design," opens with the following sentence: "The plan and style of architecture have been determined by no desire to create something unique, but are founded upon substantial reasons; they are the natural and even necessary outcome of existing conditions; the rational solution of a given problem." A pious thought, but one in conflict with several pieces of evidence. First of all, that the building is unique in that the architect, the minister, and the congregation were all well aware of what could be found in Dr. Johonnot's earlier statement, the actions of the congregation and its board of trustees, and in the very fact that the brochure was being published at all. Further, Wright seems to have been thinking about such a design and using concrete in this way for some time. Indeed, we have seen his use of it on the E-Z project. Finally, there is the written evidence of the architect's own spontaneous admission to his former colleague George Elmslie when the latter commented on the projected use for the building as a church, and Wright replied, "I don't give a damn what the use of it is; I wanted to build a building like that."[13]

The first segment after the introduction is called "The Conditions of the Problem" and describes the modest fiscal resources of the congregation and, as in the *Oak Leaves* article of February 24, makes specific reference to the cost of the other churches in the immediate vicinity and to the existence of the noisy traffic on Lake Street. The second and longer section is "How the Problem Was Solved" and justifies the use of concrete as economical, appropriate, and practical; rhetorically it derives from Wright's thinking, as later expressed in *An Autobiography*. In its praise of the "beauty of the design" (a term used twice in this section alone) and the reference to "the skill of the architect," this section does a great deal more than simply justify this particular form and style of construction, heaping praise on Wright for a building for which the stakes had only recently been set. Even were this section the particular handiwork of the architect, one wonders why the other members of the committee failed to temper the prose.

The third and final section, "The Edifice Expressive of the Faith," is a rewording and amplification of Dr. Johonnot's comments in the above-mentioned newspaper story, repeating his reference to Charles DeKay and listing the principles of liberal Christianity that he feels are represented by the building. The tone and setting in the religious framework is clearly that of the minister; none of Wright's justifications and explanations come close to such a statement as: "The attempt has been made not merely to create a religious structure, but one that fitly embodies the principles of liberal Christianity for which this church stands. These principles may be said to be unity, truth, beauty, simplicity, freedom, and reason." Several sentences are devoted to each of these principles, with poetical rather than practical justifications provided, and the brochure concludes with:

> This building conveys the sense of dignity and permanence befitting a house of religion. It has the feeling of reverence and seems to say "The Lord is in his holy temple; let all the earth keep silence before him." It is informed by that spirit of beauty which led the Psalmist to say, "Worship the Lord in the beauty of holiness."

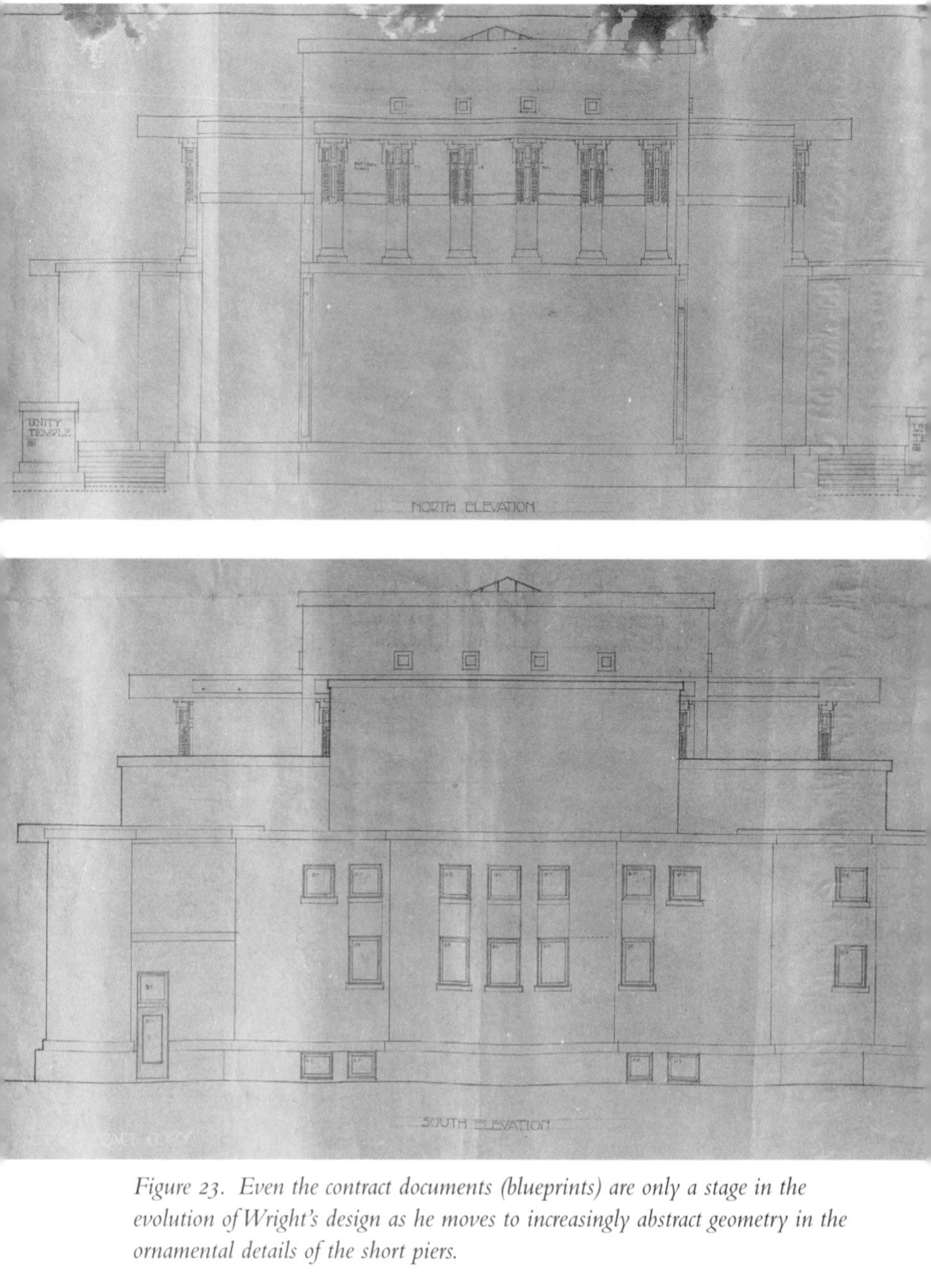

Figure 23. Even the contract documents (blueprints) are only a stage in the evolution of Wright's design as he moves to increasingly abstract geometry in the ornamental details of the short piers.

Earlier in this chapter it was suggested both that Dr. Johonnot was a man who had too much to contribute to the brochure to merely serve as Wright's mouthpiece and that his rhetoric, high flown though it may have been, reflected ideas perfectly compatible with those being expressed in the Midwestern enclaves of the Universalist Church. And, while we must recognize both that the minister had been ordained in the Universalist movement and that the church within the parish that had been organized in 1882 was affiliated with that denomination, we cannot ignore the fact that the minority group within the parish, the Unitarians, were Midwest Unitarians who identified with Jenkin Lloyd Jones and the Western Unitarian Conference, rather than with the Boston-based American Unitarian Association, whose churches were more likely to emulate the New England structure of which Wright had written.[14] Given those realities, and the importance of Jones and other Midwest ministers' positions on the subject of church architecture, it is important for us to examine the attitudes toward the church building as an institution, within both the Universalist and the Unitarian denominations, at the turn of the century.

It was the attitudes of two Unitarian ministers, Frank Lloyd Wright's uncle, Jenkin Lloyd Jones, and his Hinsdale colleague, William Channing Gannett (1840–1923), who were most influential on the reform movement in church architecture in the Midwest in the score of years preceding the construction of Unity Temple, and their ideas were important to both the minister and the architect. Gannett was an influential author, best known for his 1887 statement on liberal religion, "The Things Most Commonly Believed Today Among Us," and his description of and belief in the civilizing role of the American home in his series of sermons on the subject of "The House Beautiful," first given and published in book form in 1895 and reissued in a deluxe, hand-printed edition by William Winslow and Frank Lloyd Wright in 1896–1897. Jones, who has been described as "the most powerful western figure in the denomination,"[15] was the leader of the Western Unitarian

Alliance from 1875 to 1884, the founding minister of All Souls Church in Chicago from 1882 to 1905, and the founding director of the Abraham Lincoln Center in Chicago from 1905 to 1918.[16] Both men had rejected the traditional forms of ecclesiastical architecture in the designs produced for their congregations in the 1880s, as they

> began to challenge the hegemony of the Gothic by housing their congregations in more down-to-earth structures that enunciated the democratic religion and universal community on which the free church was based. Gannett had sought to embody these ideas in the functional quarters he helped design for his congregation in Hinsdale, Illinois, and Jones had created his own, bolder version of the church home by combining the practical features of an office building, apartment house, music hall, and gymnasium.[17]

Such a description indicates both the rejection of the Gothic style of the destroyed building and some of the rhetoric behind Wright's explanation of a multipurpose structure. In fact, his uncle's statement, *The Ideal Church*, rejected "a Gothic sham" that "promoted the sense of individual insignificance that served authoritarianism and medieval superstition," and suggested instead "a secular hall, a workshop oratory of the Soul all in one."[18] While some traditionalists among the liberal clergy opposed both Jones's ideas and the church he built in 1887, many of the Universalists in the Midwest approved of his example. Women among the clergy, in particular, viewed traditional Gothic design as an expression of patriarchal authority and instead supported Jones's identification of the church and the home. Putting it in more positive theological terms, support of the women who led the many Universalist congregations in Iowa, Wisconsin, and Michigan, "of a less aristocratic idiom was also a way of promoting a devotional language that better expressed the egalitarian ideal on which their liberal movement was founded."[19]

And while the minister of Unity Church was not part of the women's radical movement within the Universalist Church, we have already noted that his predecessor, Augusta Chapin, had been both one of their great models and a close associate of Jenkin Lloyd Jones. Liberal ideology, the identification of home and church, an anti-Gothic sentiment on egalitarian grounds, and the belief in the importance of the individual within the church were all part of the background of the Unity Church parish at the time it hired Wright to design their new building.

Thus we can identify two complementary strands in the brochure, Wright's appeal to reason and the rational grounds for both shaping the building and using the new material, concrete, in the way that was planned, and Dr. Johonnot's explanation and explication of the spiritual values being expressed through the buildings. And through the blending of the two strains, the minister's Universalist religious convictions and Wright's no-less-passionate affirmation of man's abilities, they created a very powerful statement, even if neither focused nor completely congruent. Ultimately, Wright knew what he wanted to build, and he used whatever rhetoric he had at his considerable verbal command to design what he wanted, and Dr. Johonnot was able to translate the words, and the comments about man-centered religion, into the framework that his combination of Unitarian and Universalist theology found acceptable.

While it is hard to gauge the effect of the pamphlet or the rhetoric behind it on the congregation, it is worth repeating that all of the comments that suggested concerns were based on the materials, the size and placement of windows, and the lighting. It seems that both the liberal wing of Unitarianism and the less theologically bound Universalists were really open to—if not necessarily excited about—Wright's distinctive design.

CHAPTER 4

BUILDING UNITY
TEMPLE, PART I

With the drawings complete and construction essentially assured by mid–March, the Wrights found the time for some socializing within the church community. The members of Unity Club, a social organization that had been founded in January of that year, were invited to a "Japanese Social" at the Wright's home, where those in attendance were treated to an evening of entertainment, food, and exposure to the large collection of Japanese prints the architect had purchased on a recent trip to Japan with his Highland Park clients, the Willits. The Wrights paid for the evening, and the ten cents charged each member was paid to Unity Club. Although the Wrights might have had social relationships with individual members of the church, there is no other indication of their participation in any formal activities, social or religious, with the congregation.[1] Indeed, the Wrights' local circle of friends seems to have excluded anyone other than several of his Oak Park and River Forest clients of whom he had close relations: Mr. and Mrs. Edward Waller, Mr. and Mrs. W.H. Winslow, Mr. and Mrs. Chauncey Williams, and Mr. and Mrs. Martin (for a while), to name the ones with whom we have the most knowledge. There might have been another

Figure 24. Wright had admired Japanese art and architecture since Chicago's Columbian Exposition in 1893. He bought Japanese prints on his first trip to Japan in 1905 and throughout his life. This work, Clear Weather after Snow at Kameyama *by Utagawa Hiroshige, is from Wright's private collection.*

reason for having the social, as Wright was very much involved with ideas of architecture and design, which he had seen first-hand in Japan, supplementing and enhancing an enthusiasm he had developed as far back as his repeated visits to the Japanese exhibits at the Columbian Exposition in 1893.

Sidney Robinson has talked about the influence of Japan on Wright and this building, particularly about the "space enclosed by screens," in regard to the interior. The trip to Japan was important for other designs as well, and Robinson convincingly points out how both Unity Temple and the contemporary Yahara project incorporate Wright's new understanding and thinking. No wonder he was anxious to share his experiences with the very Unity Church members who would have to come to grip and live with his nontraditional design for their church home.

Of course, by this date, the original design of the building had changed substantially, not the least of which was the move to concrete instead of the brick found in Wright's initial design (fig. 25). The proportions had been modified as well, and Robinson has described how symmetry had been developed and matured. Structural, special, and even the ornamental aspects had all been radically transformed, making for a building even more radical than the one he had initially described to the committee that had visited him in the studio. So, by the time the congregation had to formally react to the design, most of what the building was to become could be reviewed. The material had been changed to concrete, the floor of the auditorium had been raised, the four sets of stairs had been added, the ceiling of the sanctuary had become a grid of squares, and the wood strips had changed in both placement and function.

The annual meeting of the congregation took place the next week, on March 26, and a new board of trustees took office. At the April 1 meeting of the board, William G. Adams, an attorney for the Chicago and Oak Park Elevated Railroad Company, was elected to the position of president, and he appointed the other board members to the various standing committees. John Lewis was the continuing member of the board who we have already noted to as

Figure 25. The first design for Unity Temple indicates both the exterior and the interior, in appearance much like the Larkin Building, to be made of brick. The exterior of the E-Z Polish Building had also been covered in brick, as was the Arthur Heurtley house, just down the block from Wright's own home.

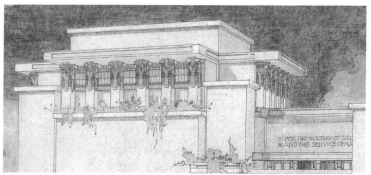

having been one of the major supporters of the new church proposal, and one of Wright's strongest allies, and he became chairman of the finance committee. And, even more important, Edwin H. Ehrman, a new board member, was appointed as chairman of the church and grounds committee.

The building committee and the architect were very busy during April, for Wright had called for bids on his completed plans and specifications and had received at least one bid based on a proposal to do the concrete work with a different finish than that called for in the specs.[2] Surprisingly, Wright was receptive, as judged by the fact that the final list of bids included the revised one by that particular firm. By the time the church board met on April 28, three bids had been received, including the revised submission of H. Eilenberger & Co., but there was really no contest. J.H. Johnson of Chicago bid $62,841, Eilenberger had lowered his to $48,459, and Paul Mueller, Wright's old colleague and the man who had provided the rough estimate for the congregation in the first place, was clearly the low bidder at $32,221. None of the bids included heating, plumbing, electrical wiring, or furniture, though Mueller actually did include the pews for the church in his low bid.

Looking back at the process, Wright described the problem in terms of lack of receptivity to his daring design:

> Now, who will build the temple? After weeks of prospecting, no one can be found who wants to try it. Simple enough—yes—that's the trouble. So simple there is nothing at all to gauge it by. Requires too much imagination and initiative to be safe. The only bids available came in double, or more, our utmost limit. No one really wanted to touch it. Contractors are naturally gamblers but they usually bet on a sure thing—as they see the thing.
>
> Paul Mueller comes to the rescue, reads the scheme like easy print. Will build it for only a little over their appropriation—and does it....Doesn't lose much on it in the end.[3]

As we have already seen, Mueller had already provided the estimate for the board of trustees and, while we have nothing from his own hand to corroborate his early involvement in the project, he had obviously seen Wright's plans at an early stage of design. Thus, it is fatuous for Wright to describe him as coming to the rescue; he was in on the bidding from the very beginning, and, indeed, had a head start on the other general contractors. With these advantages and both his prior and contemporary experience in working with Wright on several buildings, and even in the essentially new medium of concrete with the E-Z Polish project, it is hardly surprising that he felt confident in bidding on the innovative proposal. On the other hand, as he knew the way the architect worked and his propensity for design change full well, we can reasonably wonder how Mueller thought he could complete the work within the budget.

Perhaps the answer to this lies in the many projects on which the two men were working at the time. Not only had Mueller just finished work on the Larkin Building and the E-Z Polish factory (a joint project of Darwin Martin of Buffalo and W. Martin of Oak Park), but he was also working on several other large Wright homes in both Chicago and Buffalo, for the Martin brothers and others related to the Larkin Company. Clearly the two men understood each other and had the greatest trust in each other, as Mueller was also to later lead the team that built two major and gigantic projects for Wright, both Midway Gardens, and even later, the Imperial Hotel in Japan. That is not to say that Mueller necessarily believed that Unity Temple could be built within the budget, but he did believe in Wright and his ability to make things happen. However, as Paul Mueller turned out to be an extremely poor correspondent who left neither records of his office nor autobiographical writings, we have no way of knowing what he thought he was facing on this particular project. As we shall see, it couldn't be done for the price he quoted, and in the end, Mueller lost more than Wright could or would admit.

In any case, we have already noted the meeting on the night of the 28th, after the president reported the results of the bidding to the entire board, Mr. Lewis, pushing as hard as ever to begin construction, moved a resolution accepting the eight pages of drawings and the forty-one of plans and specifications as submitted by the architect. After that was approved, it was moved that a sense of the meeting indicate the intention to proceed with the construction of the entire building. It is worth repeating that the minister proposed to the board that a meeting of the Church Society be called to "pass on the question of the erection of the church edifice entire or in part."[4] Whether the minister was speaking for himself or was, perhaps, responding to a last-ditch attempt on the part of Mr. Skillin cannot be determined, but the board had no interest in further debate, with a "motion made and carried to place Dr. Johonnot's letter on file."[5] The sense of the meeting resolution then passed. Mr. Lewis then moved the acceptance of Paul Mueller's low bid of $32,221 under contract to the board, provided he agree to and provide a performance bond in the amount of $15,000. The motion was approved, and the president was directed to execute such a contract on behalf of the board. Several questions were raised, including the exact position of the building on the lot, and the board agreed to adjourn to a meeting to be held at the architect's office on the night of the 30th.

Both Wright and Mueller responded to the board member's questions that Monday evening, and apparently resolved their doubts about all of the matters under discussion, except the location of the building on the long, narrow lot. However, the general contractor was unwilling to sign the contract that the board had approved and submitted to him. He had been out of town overseeing another job being handled by his growing firm—a firm with branches in Buffalo and Cleveland at that date—and, as the board minutes clearly indicate, had not responded to the call for bids personally. As the board secretary was to note: "but Mr. Mueller, having had no opportunity to go over the estimates of his engineer was not prepared to sign a contract, and the board adjourned to the next evening at the same location."[6] Paul Mueller, having examined the contract that day, had discovered that his firm's bid did not include several items (unfortunately, neither the board minutes nor the correspondence indicate which items were involved), and that there was a discrepancy of $440. After some discussion, Mr. Lewis proposed a successful motion to have the president execute a contract with Mueller in the new amount of $32,661. The requirement for the $15,000 completion bond was to remain unchanged, and the building was to be completed by November 15 of that same year! Through all of this, Lewis was clearly the most vocal and forceful of Wright's supporters, again making us wonder why he is totally absent from the architect's narrative.

The board of trustees held their regular May meeting on the sixth and discussed several matters related to the new building. First, they took up the important matter of raising major funds for the building, with John Lewis reporting for the finance committee. He had brought a list of members who had not been contributing to the regular operating expenses of the church, but with the expenses of using the borrowed facility so low, it was decided not to pursue them for the moment. Instead, because it was deemed more important to concentrate on soliciting subscriptions to the building fund, each board member selected those he wished to call upon from a list of names prepared by the finance committee. As part of the same committee report, it was decided to pay the taxes due on part of the recently acquired property from the monies in the building fund and to commit up to $80 for Mueller's builder's bond from the same source.

Charles Roberts was then invited in to participate in the ongoing discussion of the placement of the building on the lot, a discussion necessitated by the length of the building on a long and narrow lot, and with the long side facing a side, rather than a main, street. We do not know which alternatives were discussed, but it is recorded that the board finally decided "that the church edifice be so placed on the lot that there be a space of three feet between the South foundation at grade and the South line of the lot."[7] As the building was to be 144 feet long, that left twenty-three feet of open space between the building and the sidewalk on the side that faced the main street, Lake Street, while the building occupies the entire width of the lot. However, as there is a walkway to the entrances on both the east and west sides of the building, those entering the terraced areas and viewers on the north side are given a transition of space before encountering the mass of the building's width.

At the same meeting at which the commitments as to siting were finalized, both Ed Ehrman and C.A. Sharpe were officially added to the building committee. Given the multiple roles and the time commitment that Ehrman was to play over the next several years, that decision was to have far-reaching consequences.

With the siting issue finally resolved, the first real step in the construction process could take place, and after the architect and builder met to discuss details of the process, the stakes were set on Saturday, May 12. Wright had recently hired his brother-in-law, A.L. Tobin, to handle the business affairs of the firm, and it was Tobin who notified President Adams that the stakes had been set and that they were ready to pour the concrete.[8] The architect also submitted his bill for architectural services at the same time.

The church board met in special session on May 20 to discuss procedures and finances. They agreed to pay Wright $1,243.23, roughly 80 percent of the architect's fee, and authorized the treasurer to issue the first certificate in that amount. In regard to procedures, it was agreed that the building committee would supervise the construction of the new church with the broad authority and powers to insure completion of the project within schedule. Further, it fell on the chairman of the committee to approve the certificates submitted by the architect before the treasurer would pay the contractors for whom they were issued, though another member of the building committee could sign in his absence.[9] Thus, the major responsibility for overseeing construction and approving the quality of the work fell on the shoulders of the building committee chairman. When Charles Roberts resigned that position, less than two weeks later, that major responsibility was placed with Edwin H. Ehrman.

Ehrman had joined the church in 1889 and was a partner in Walker and Ehrman Manufacturing Company, a firm that, at the time of his appointment to the board, had been absorbed into Charles Roberts's Chicago Screw Company and for which he served as factory manager and corporate secretary. Wearing the two hats most critical to the construction of the new church, those of chairman of both the board's church and grounds committee and the building committee, and combining business and managerial experience with absolute dedication to the congregation and the project at hand, Ed Ehrman was to be the single most important representative of the church in seeing the building through to completion. He was to spend countless hours in handling the affairs of the church, in dealing with the architect, the builder, and the problems with the many subcontractors working on the building; he had to approve the quality and cost of the work, had to approve payment, and managed to even serve as the conciliator when the inevitable and the avoidable conflicts arose between the church board and any of the other parties.

The amount of wood necessary to create the forms was substantial, and the amount of concrete formidable, with the building some thirty feet in height over the sanctuary. Wright's brilliant design decision was to make the major sections of the building of the same dimensions, thereby enabling the reuse of the timber that provided the frame for the concrete pours, each section of panel to contain the concrete being twelve feet long and three and one-half feet tall. Yet the many shapes of stairway areas, the entrance sections, and other parts of the building were substantial and of a very different scale from the major piers and walls, necessitating additional work and lumber.

Ehrman and his committee had a lot to do almost immediately as the very first step in the construction process, pouring the

Figure 26. Ed Ehrman became the principal player in working with Wright, the contractor, and the congregation. He was the person who balanced egos, schedules, budgets, and showed almost endless tact and patience. His contributions to Unity Temple were lifelong. Courtesy Unity Temple Restoration Foundation

foundation footings, presented a problem. The specifications provided by the architect pointed to a slow process, with the requirement that the poured foundations were to rise at no greater a rate than one foot, six inches in a twenty-four-hour period, in an attempt to ensure proper setting.[10] However, the committee was unpleasantly surprised by the concrete contractor informing them that extra excavation work would be needed and that it would take more concrete than had been estimated to complete the foundations. Nonetheless, the board acknowledged that the work was necessary and later approved the increased expenditure of $172.50 for the additional excavation and $473.10 for pouring the additional concrete, for a total of $645.60. In the future, board members found themselves less likely to approve variations from the original specifications and plans and usually were unwilling to pay for the expensive changes suggested by the architect after the building was under construction.

Another matter that slowed down construction, at the beginning, was the extended absence of Mueller in June, which prevented him from completing and signing the performance bond required by the terms of the contract.[11] Though it is easy to blame the novelty of the materials and the architect's frequent mid-construction changes for much of the slow progress toward the building's completion, there were also other factors at work. Paul Mueller was often at work in other parts of the country and, in the early days of the project, was usually in Buffalo completing the Larkin Building and several Wright projects for homes there. So, when there were problems to be resolved at the Unity Temple site, his absence did not help move things along. Consequently, when construction either halted or slowed down substantially later on, for whatever cause, it became easy for the board to express its frustration in terms of the absence of the contractor.

The large quantity of concrete necessary for the foundation was upsetting to the board but was no cause for confrontation with either Wright or Mueller. However, a matter like suggesting a change in the finish of the exterior of the building, the subject of a letter of July 10 Wright sent to the board, produced a different kind of response (the letter below, and all following, are reproduced as written, with errors):

Hoping to secure the best possible finish for the exterior of the new building some experiments have been worked out at the site and your attention is now respectfully called to the same.

Exhibit o-1 conforms to the specifications, and o-o-1, o-2, o-3 are variations of the same type, all floted.

In Exhibit A-1, and others similar, finely screened gravel has been used instead of the crushed granite, and instead of the floting the surface subsequently treated with a preparation bringing the gravel into relief.

Finished according to Exhibit A-1 the surface would be as durable as o-1 and perhaps much richer, probably a more desirable surface for your building. The gravel is in itself some cheaper than the crushed granite but the carefur screening necessary to a good result makes it somewhat more expensive. The subsequent washing of the surface will consume rather more time than the floting but the contractor prefers the A-1 method because the risk in obtaining a uniform result will be less than in the method originally specified.

The chemically treated surface being a more dependable quantity than the floted in the hands of indifferent or even in the hands of careful workmen, as no two men produce surfaces entirely alike.

There would be no difference made in the cost of the work to the Trustees if the work proceed according to method A-1.

Inasmuch as it is expedient to begin filling the boxes by the 16th of this month, unless objection is previously urged by them the work will proceed according to A-1.[12]

Robinson has noted that Wright wanted to use crushed red granite on the walls of the exterior, and that he was proposing it for the wrong architectural reason of holding on to the traditional architectural division of base, wall, and cornice. The scholar has noted what the architect only later came to see, that the rejection of the red granite on economic grounds ended up creating the monolithic and unified building that Unity Temple came to be. Indeed, it is hard to imagine the effect of the proposed two-tone building, and it is obvious that the solidity and massing of the structure would have been diluted by the mix of colors. Equally as important, part of the majesty and importance of Unity Temple is the rejection of that kind of traditional demarcation of the three parts: circumstances and economics conspired to create a modern building that broke free of twenty-five hundred years of building traditions.

It is worth noting Ehrman's response to Wright's wishes and proposal, as an indication of the difference of opinion and as an excellent example of the thoroughness, seriousness, and expertise he brought to his commitment of the church and the job at hand. Although he was about to leave town for a summer vacation, after reading Wright's letter and carefully examining the samples at the site, Ehrman sent the following to the president of the board:[13]

> I presume you will have a meeting to change the specifications so as to conform to Mr. Wright's change in exterior finish. As I leave for Mich. tonight I have listed my choice & should there be any opportunity for a vote you may express mine as follows,—
>
> 1st choice 06 trowel finish
>
> 2nd " 02 trowel & flote
>
> 3rd " A3 this is preferable to A1 & A2 on a/c of fineness
>
> *last* choice A1
>
> I cannot understand why he has thrown out 01, not making a sample till the last thing and then not attempting to finish it as he has the others,—(it was molded *flat* not on edge and was not given a flote finish at all.
>
> I think the sample A1 is poor and A2 but little better. A3 is better than either.
>
> I like 02 (brush & flote finish) but its looks like the common cement plaster on metal lath.
>
> I am afraid of his choice unless they are very careful in finishing the surface. The only thing to my mind that commends it is that it is different from what others have done.[14]

There were also financial problems created by this experiment and change in treatment, as there were by each of the many on-site changes proposed (or directly ordered) by the architect, though this was one of those major ones that only surfaced when bills were later submitted by Mueller. Wright got the board to agree to his change in surface, but they were later to refuse to pay Mueller for the cost of either the creation of the twenty samples ($343.75) or for the change from concrete faced with birdseye to reinforced

Figure 27. This construction photograph shows the all-important wooden forms that were used for the concrete construction. The process was necessarily slow, as "pours" were to take place at a maximum of one foot, six inches, every twenty-four hours, to ensure proper setting.

solid birdseye ($2,732.80), citing Wright's letter of July 10 and his statement that there would be no additional cost to the church.[15]

The walls went up slowly, as the forms had to be taken down and reconstructed as each new section was built and the painstaking method of construction was followed: Wright specified that the surface mortar should be directly trowelled onto the interior faces of the molds, to a minimum thickness of one and one-half inches before the body of concrete was filled in behind and thoroughly tamped. All of this took much longer than simply pouring concrete, and even the exterior work on Unity House was far from complete by November 15, the date set by the contract for completion of the entire project. Over two and a half years were to elapse before the structure was substantially complete, and many changes of plans and the architect's choice of materials were to create problems that caused both cost overruns and completion delays, but the basic concrete work had to be done very slowly, so as not to threaten the stability of the entire structure!

As the building gradually took shape, the building committee turned its attention to the plumbing, heating, and electrical systems. After some months of negotiations and similar hesitations about the appropriateness of the contractor, a contract was issued for Foster & Glidden Co., of Oak Park, for "Heating and Ventilating Systems, Plumbing and Electrical Wiring" on September 24, 1906. The scope of the work had already been defined in the initial specifications drawn up by the architect, and they were referenced in the contract. F & G were to be paid $3,400 and posted a performance bond in the amount of $1,500. A special meeting of the church board was called on September 30, as the contract had not been signed by the church. Mr. Ehrman noted that "Foster & Glidden had already performed work and furnished materials on account of said work to the value of at least $300," and had the board agree to pay them $250 with the proviso that the payment would be applied to any contract eventually negotiated with F & G.[16] Isabel Roberts, Wright's secretary, wrote President Adams on October 2, informing him that the contract was ready for the board's action. There were problems with the firm's specs, however, and the matter was repeatedly deferred. A subcommittee of Ehrman and Charles Roberts was delegated to handle the matter. At the regular board meeting for December, it was agreed to meet at Wright's studio on December 5 to consider the bid and, upon the recommendation of the subcommittee, it was finally approved. Interestingly enough, though Ehrman had replaced him, Roberts seems to have remained involved for some period of time, before practically disappearing from the narrative completely.

Work on the building itself continued to move slowly, and Mueller's repeated and sometimes lengthy trips to other parts of the country did little to help the situation. On January 30, 1907, the exasperated chairman of the building committee, Ehrman, finally penned a strong letter to the builder, defining not only the frustration felt by the committee and board, but also the negative impact on the entire congregation:

> Confirming my conversation a week ago over the telephone with your engineer, I am calling your attention to the rather slow progress being made on "Unity House" at present....The truth of the matter is that not a few of our people are discouraged and finding the payments on subscriptions very slow. The people want to see where the money is going and what they are going to get in return, and the committee has never been able to give them any satisfactory information as to when any part of the Church would be completed.[17]

Ehrman's preferred form of meeting problems with the project was to request information or compliance in the most gentle and well-mannered way, but, especially when failing to get an answer to his requests, he could throw down an economic gauntlet. His letter continued:

> Up to the present we have been prompt in meeting your vouchers as presented, but we can see that in the near future we can not do this unless some immediate showing is made on the part of the contractors. You will make our committee and yourself as well, a great deal of trouble if the work continues as slowly as it has the past three or four weeks.
>
> I requested a letter from your office last week, but you had not returned from New Orleans by the 26th to give the matter attention.

> Now, conditions are such that we ought have a state-
> ment from you, something definite that we can *depend* on,
> as to when and how soon we can expect to have the use
> of Unity House. In a month we shall hold our annual
> parish meeting, and we must be able to meet in our new
> building.[18]

He concludes with a more plaintive appeal for cooperation:

> If on account of the building not being completed (inside)
> we cannot hold this meeting in it, we are going to suffer
> there from in more ways than one…if we have to pass
> by another annual parish meeting this next month as
> we did a year ago, it will seriously tend to demoralize our
> Society.…Let me receive from you in time to make pub-
> lic on Sunday a letter stating definitely that the building
> will be ready for occupancy as requested above.[19]

Building projects have almost always taken longer than
planned, and the fact that some of the issues here were not exclusively of the architect's (or even the builder's) doing were never
noted by those frustrated by the process. We don't know if there
were any strikes in the trades in Chicago at that time, or if there
were ever a shortage of supplies or skilled workmen, but we do
know that both Wright and Mueller had other irons in the fire.

Yet Ehrman was not the only one worried about the slow pace
of construction and the difficulty of motivating members to support
the project. On October 9, President Adams sent his quarterly contribution of $12.50 with a letter asking the treasurer for a list of sub-
scribers who had yet to honor their commitments; he wished to
call upon them personally. At the board of trustees' regular November meeting, moreover, "It was considered best to have all those seen
in person whose subscriptions to the church fund were due and
unpaid & Mr. Lewis, the Pres, & Treas took lists of such names."[20]

With the new church far from complete and after a long period in rented quarters, the financial situation was fairly grim: membership had substantially declined since the fire, yet the heavy expenses of paying for both construction and a rented facility were growing. The treasurer's report at the February board meeting included a general fund balance of \$73.14 and projected a deficit by the end of the fiscal quarter. The board members found themselves in the difficult position of continuing to press for subscription payments as agreed upon two months earlier and considering an additional subscription to make up the deficit. It was decided that, at least for the time being, priority should be given to collecting on the overdue building fund obligations. Efforts were made in that direction with the result that the general fund balance dipped even further and totalled only \$11.31 at the time of the March meeting.

Progress on the building did pick up, though not sufficiently to enable the congregation to meet there in March. On February 3, the board voted that "the Building Committee have a monolith floor placed in the entrance hall and in Unity House."[21] The heating system was also installed in February, though final adjustments were not yet completed: Ehrman was anxious for work to continue but reluctant to have the heating system going unless the builder would take the responsibility for it while his subcontractors worked inside. He wrote Mueller on February 23, "As the matter stands there is no objection to your making use of the plant, in fact we would rather have you use it than have it lie idle. It must be understood, however, that you will assume the entire responsibility so long as you make use of it for heating the building in order to carry on your work."[22]

We know that work was slow primarily because of the divided workload of not only Paul Mueller's office, but several of the other contractors having major commitments elsewhere, including Buffalo, New York—Wright had not brought only Mueller in to the several homes that were part of the spin-off of the Larkin Building. And winter weather certainly didn't help, in spite of the willingness of the congregation to allow the building to be heated while everyone worked. Mueller and his cohorts were no different than contractors seem always to have been, both in the earlier twentieth century, and today, taking on as many jobs as they could contract, and then taking a path somewhere between giving priority to either the most lucrative project or the squeakiest wheel, and trying to keep all projects going at an equal (but slow) rate.

With all the delays and frustrations over both time and financial matters, as already described, Ehrman, as head of the building committee, wrote the architect about both matters almost two weeks before the scheduled annual congregational meeting. The tone of the interchange between the earnest and worried board member and the unruffled architect is caught so clearly in the letters that it is important to compare them. Ehrman wrote:

> Dear Sir:
>
> Our committee will have to present to the members of the parish information as to the additional cost of work on the new church not already covered by contract.
>
> We would be pleased therefore to have *accurate* estimates and other data as noted below. We would suggest that where possible bids be obtained so as to avoid revision later when the time comes to proceed with the work.
>
> Monolith Floor Unity House—(1) area—sq.ft.
>
> (2) price per sq. fit.
>
> (3) allowance made for omitting top dressing of concrete floor.
>
> Lettering—(1) words and location.
>
> (2) cost per word or lot.
>
> Light Fixtures—(1) number and distribution.
>
> (2) price each or for lot.
>
> Outside Lights—(1) location and nature. (2) cost each (or lot). Organ Screen—(1) cost
>
> Cement Walks—(1) area in sq. ft.

(2) price per square foot.

Grading—(1) nature.

(2) estimate or estimates.

We should be able to present information concerning the above work to the board not later than Thursday.

We are very much encouraged with the progress made of late on the interior finishing work in Unity House. It would appear now that with the ground puddled and graded and with the roof completed, that Mr. Mueller ought to be able to make rapid headway, and we would be gratified to be able to give to the parish at our annual meeting this coming week some definite information as to when the building will be ready for occupancy.

We trust we may hear from you as requested, and would impress upon you the importance of *definite* and *accurate* information at this time in order that the trustees may obtain the necessary power to proceed with the completion of the work smoothly and without delay.

Yours very truly,

E.H. Ehrman, Chairman[23]

Wright's undated reply (probably of March 18), is casual, makes a humorous dig at Ehrman's profession, and in the last sentence—considering that he was the target of the underlined pointed comments about accurate and definite information—is disingenuous.

My dear Ed:—

No doubt you mean well and I will therefore prepare a cost schedule and a statement which I will present to the meeting myself, if you don't mind. It will be as definite and accurate as a screw.

I only hope you have not been accustomed to receiving information that is indefinite and inaccurate concerning the church. If so, will you kindly tell me who has been

responsible for it and I will see that whoever it is is properly called down.

    Yours in the same old way,

    Frank [hand signed][24]

Accompanying the letter, and likewise on letterhead, is an
item-by-item estimate for the projects as defined by Ehrman, with
the exception of the number and location of light fixtures, which
the architect felt he could not itemize at the time. Equally important, Wright stated that Unity House would be ready for occupancy by May 15 and the Temple itself would be ready by
September 1 of that year.

Armed with this information, the board of trustees and minister carefully prepared for the annual parish meeting. The secretary
was asked to send out a meeting notice, with return postage, to
each family in the congregation, and to inform the members of
the important business at hand.[25] As Unity House was not yet complete, the supper and meeting were to be held at the First Baptist
Church, near the site of their own destroyed church.

In addition to the usual reports and business, there were three
major items on the agenda. The first was to be the progress report
on construction of the new church building, the second a stronger
than usual pitch for the funds necessary to pay for the building,
and the third the election of new members of the board of trustees.
The first two items were to be expected and were certainly on the
minds of the entire congregation, but the election, simply presented
as "Four Trustees, a Secretary and Treasurer are to be elected," was
perhaps the most significant item on the agenda.

Two trustees had recently resigned; the terms of two others
were over, and neither chose to run for another term; and the long-
time secretary, Dr. Guy Parke Conger, also chose to retire. That
meant that the incoming board would not only have lost Mr. Lewis,
the most vocal and insistent supporter of Wright and the new
building, but would have only one member, President Adams (and

the treasurer) with longer than one year's service. That is not to suggest that the old anti-building forces were returning to positions of authority, for just the opposite was true. Joining the two officers and Ed Ehrman were Frank Adams and F.J. Watson for one year terms, Charles Roberts and Charles Woodard for three-year terms, and Marshall Jackson as secretary. All but Watson had been closely associated with the development of the still uncompleted church: Jackson had served with Ehrman as a member of the committee on plans; Roberts and Frank Adams had served on the building committee; Woodard had served both on the ways and means committee *and*, with the minister and the architect, on the committee on the brochure. After nine frustrating months in which almost all the pressure was on Ehrman, he now had stronger allies. These men were not only committed to the building but knew what they wanted it to be.

The reports of the various committees and auxiliary organizations were themselves tied to the finances and progress of the new church building. The superintendent of the Sunday school, for example, after reporting that $150 of the pledge to the new building had been paid "said frankly that the Sunday School was not in the most flourishing condition; it being handicapped, of course, by a Hall unfitted for the work."[26] The Ladies Social Union, on the other hand, reported an all-time-high membership of fifty-eight, with a balance of over $600 after their pledge to the building fund had been paid. And among the new members was Anna Wright, the architect's mother, perhaps as a gesture of support for the congregation and their new building.[27]

After the leaders of several other church organizations gave their reports, Dr. Johonnot delivered his fifteenth annual report, and it was even more negative than that of the Sunday school superintendent. He noted:

> [T]he average church attendance had fallen down to 85, the lowest in 15 years. While he recognized that the external

conditions of the year had been hard, he deplored the fact
that such things should have so affected the church work
and interest. He said that many had worked hard with mind,
body and spirit, but many others he feared were waiting for
the new church to awaken in them the spirit, which should
be in their hearts first.[28]

Immediately after the minister's talk, President Adams gave his
report, which, perforce, was heavily devoted to the progress and
funding of the new building. A resolution was then offered, authorizing the board of trustees to borrow as much money as necessary
to insure the completion of the new church edifice and to mort-
gage the property if they deemed it appropriate. The resolution was
moved and seconded, but the conservatives, once again led by
Skillin, opposed the move toward indebtedness. He wanted more
time for the parish to consider such a move, in the hopes that some
other plan might relieve them of the necessity of borrowing money.
In an answer reminiscent of those he previously used to argue with
the then president about the issue of constructing the entire edifice versus a phased project, Skillin's old antagonist Lewis showed
willingness to wait a few days before coming to a final decision,
while clearly indicating his opposition to the former's position:

Some pledges are not due and some will come in slowly
and the needs could be met only with ready money. The
board had been given authority to build the New Church
and after long and careful consideration had decided to
build the entire building and had so let the contracts. He
thought they must borrow such amount as were necessary.
Believed the total amount would be pledged by the time
the building was completed.[29]

After some additional discussion, the resolution was deferred to
a special meeting to be called by the board; it was soon scheduled

for April 1 at the same board meeting at which President Adams was unanimously reelected to that position. The issue of borrowing was then carefully discussed at the adjourned meeting and passed unanimously.

The actions taken at the annual meeting were widely known, thanks to a front-page story in the Saturday, March 30, edition of *Oak Leaves*, that reported the election results and commented that "the finances were in good condition, tho considerable money yet remains to be pledged to cover the whole cost of building. To this end another canvass of the parish will be made in the near future." The same story reported Wright's estimate as to the dates of completion for the two parts of the building, and referenced President Adams's conciliatory remark that "the delay in finishing the work had been due to many unexpected causes without fault on the part of the contractor."[30]

An interesting sidelight is provided on the same page in the newspaper where it is reported that T.J. Skillin and a Charles Richards were likely to be renominated and possibly reelected as school board trustees, though they would be facing opposition from an unrepresented eighth precinct. Clearly Mr. Skillin spent much time in public service, even serving on such ad hoc committees (and in this case with Mr. Lewis) as was the one appointed to consider amendments to the by-laws, and so charged at the April meeting of the board of trustees.[31]

The April board meeting and all those through the month of August were held at the studio of the architect Charles White Jr., a new member of the church and the former Wright associate who had so vividly commented on the struggle for acceptance of the plans by the board committee just a year earlier. It is not known why the board met at his studio, other than for reasons of proximity to the church and convenience, as White was neither a member of any relevant committee nor does he figure in any of the minutes of the discussions that were held in his space. All of the board's working committees were established at the April meeting and, not surprisingly, Ed Ehrman was reappointed as chair of the church and grounds committee; Charles Roberts joined him as the other member of the two-person committee and himself took on the chairmanship of the finance committee, backed up by Charles Woodard.

The other item relating to ongoing work on the building was a motion authorizing Wright to order metal letters and squares to be placed over the entrances of the new church, subject to the approval of the committee; $225 was voted for this purpose. The addition of a new, though admittedly minor, expense at a time when the congregation was finding it difficult to meet its existing obligations was something that was to be repeated many times before the building was completed. We shall see that many of Wright's ideas were rejected and, as with the change in surface finishing, the board demurred about paying for additional work that they had been told would have no cost. And even when new expenses were approved, as in this lettering issue, the already gun-shy board at least attempted to have committee oversight and approval of the specifics.

By the time of the May meeting, it was apparent that the decision to borrow money would have to be implemented. The general fund had a balance of $11.69, but the excess of liabilities over resources produced a deficit of $298.81. With all the attempts to secure payment on subscriptions, pledges, etc., it had only been decreased by about $10 by the time the board met in June. A total balance sheet on the Building Fund was presented at that meeting, showing $22,582.85 already paid to Mueller and Foster & Glidden, and $13,078.15 yet to be paid. With $2,159.24 available in the fund as a result of subscription payments, an Easter collection, and the remains of the original fund, the trustees voted to "borrow of the Oak Park Trust and Savings Bank the sum of Four thousand Dollars at the current rate of interest...to become payable on demand."[32] The money was borrowed and first appears in the Treasurer's Report for the month of August, with an interest due of $59.33.

Work was progressing on both parts of the new edifice, with the major attention being paid to the completion of Unity House. The May 15 promised completion date had come and gone, but with good weather ahead, all involved came to hope and believe that at least Unity House would be ready for congregational use by the start of the fall session of services. Ehrman was trying to get Mueller to speed the contractors on to completion and, at the same time, attempting to make the building and grounds visually presentable. He wrote the architect on June 11, asking that he make sure that dirt and rubbish was removed, and that he direct the contractor "to discontinue throwing rubbish out of the windows, as the dust from this has also been the cause for complaint." Another aspect of aesthetic concern was to be addressed by giving permission to "have the out house cleared away and install one of the closets in Unity House for the use of the men in its stead."[33] Interestingly and significantly, considering that Wright had so recently given a completion date of September 1 for the entire project, Ehrman's letter goes on to imply that he does not expect the work to be done for the better part of another year: "The aspect of our building in its present condition is not very inviting, and inasmuch as the neighbors will have had to endure it for two years, we should be careful about annoying them as possible." His unofficial estimate was to be surprisingly accurate.

By the time the board of trustees met for their postponed monthly meeting in late August, the building committee could see that a few additional weeks were needed before they could begin to use Unity House even for services. Thus, the board accepted their recommendation that the resumption of services be delayed and a notice be sent all congregants announcing that the first service in Unity House would be on September 15. At the same time, "The building committee was given authority to look after coal and light contracts and the vestry committee to hire janitor and provide for cleaning."[34] Mueller, himself, acknowledged that the

Temple would not be completed for some time to come and provided access to Unity House when he sent the following carefully worded letter to the building committee:

> Inasmuch as I have not been able to fulfill my contract and complete Unity Church by the date called for therein, and inasmuch as part of the building, known as Unity House, is ready for occupancy, permission is hereby given Unity Church Society to occupy said Unity House temporarily until the entire building shall have been completed and accepted, under the following conditions:—
>
> First—The occupancy of said Unity House shall not be construed as in any manner whatever affecting the contract now existing between Unity Church and Paul F.P. Mueller. Second—Said occupancy shall not in any way be construed as being an acceptance of said building or any part of it.[35]

Clearly, not only was the building not complete by the time designated in the original contract nor by the date projected by the architect a few months earlier, but no new date was even projected for completion at this time.

The pastor's letter announcing the first service in the new edifice was mailed on September 4 and stated:

> After more than two years of waiting since the burning of our former edifice, we can now meet in our own church home. Unity House is now ready for use, and while not designed primarily as a place of public worship, it will serve for this purpose fairly well and will give us fitting accommodations for all other church activities.[36]

CHAPTER 5

BUILDING UNITY TEMPLE, PART II

The first service in Unity House was held on Sunday, September 15, 1907, and the congregation turned out in force. The press provided a full account of the response to the building, and the lead sentence in the *Oak Leaves* story underscored the the church members' emotions:

> It was a very happy lot of people that assembled at Unity House last Sunday morning, for the members of Unity church were once more housed under their own roof for the first time for over two years. These months of waiting heightened the joy of the occasion. The house, which will seat about 250 people, was filled to every seat....Many remained at the close of the service to inspect the building and expressions of delight and satisfaction were universal.[1]

Moreover, the same story provides the earliest recorded description of the contrast between the exterior and the interior, including specific information on the long-disputed colors of the interior:

> The surfaces of the room are broken by paneling, thus
> affording opportunity for using different colors in the tint-
> ing of the walls which is taken advantage of by the use of
> browns, light greens, and yellows. The woodwork is of
> unpolished oak, which blends finely with the prevailing
> tone of the brown tinting....The severe simplicity of the
> exterior of the building, especially in its present unfinished
> state, gives one little hint of the beauty of the interior and
> its beauty came quite as a revelation to all who had not
> visited it before the service.[2]

The Ladies Social Union held their first meeting in Unity House the same week and were pleased with the appearance of their new quarters. They voted to spend their available funds on accessories for the new building, committing to the purchase of fifty chairs for Unity House and for steam tables and gas stoves for the new kitchen.[3]

It is evident that the close-to-complete Unity House was extremely well received, and hopes were high for the prompt com- pletion of the Temple as well, but it was to be two full years of anx- iety, frustration, and added expense before the building was, indeed, completed and dedicated. And, as work progressed on both the building and its furnishings, the problems overlapped and became more complex. For the most part, Ed Ehrman was to continue to bear not only the responsibility but, as is made amply clear through even a casual examination of his correspondence with both Wright and Mueller, often even parts of the expense of the new building. Though he tried to be a tough businessman, as in the previously quoted letter to Wright in which he had demanded a strict accounting as to deadlines, the chairman of the building commit- tee always came down on the side of kindness.

One of the several examples of the way Ehrman let his heart rule his head is seen in the exchange of letters that documents both his frustration with the architect's lack of adherence to established procedures and his personal response in regard to the workmen caught unawares in the middle. With a memo in hand from William Drummond (then serving as Wright's superintendent, and later an important Oak Park Prairie School architect in his own right), listing the basic costs of light fixtures for Unity House and containing an explanation for the need to pay the carpenter who installed them, Ehrman wrote to Wright on September 24:

> I would be pleased to have your complete estimate for these fixtures in both Unity Temple and Unity House. This will be acted on by the board at its next meeting Oct. 1st and it will be necessary to have the board's action before I can pass on any more vouchers, so you will see the advisability of mailing me your estimate before that date.
>
> Before your estimate a Mr. Bauer called with a certificate for $46.50 and was much disappointed because he could not get the money at once. I have since mailed him my personal check for the amount in order to save him further inconvenience, but cannot make a practice of so doing.

In the same letter, Ehrman also made an additional pitch for playing by the rules by concluding:

> It will be apparent then that all of the minor jobs should take the regular course of being approved and an order obtained before proceeding to their execution, in order that we may all be saved the annoyance that is sure to otherwise occur.[4]

The records don't make clear whether getting an estimate for the wall fixtures proved difficult, but the October meeting came and went with no additional information provided by the architect. It was only in conjunction with the issuance of certificates for the rest of the job that Wright sent Ehrman a schedule of complete cost on January 18, 1908. The chairman of the building committee was to demand schedules, certificates, and prior approval, time and time again, but was often to pay—several additional times out of his own pocket—when faced with a subcontractor who expected and wanted to be paid for his work upon its satisfactory completion. In addition, when there were inevitable minor misunderstandings and/or small adjustments to be made, either to ensure the goodwill of the complaining party or to take the path of least resistance, Ehrman also resorted to assuming obligations addressed to the congregation. Thus, when Foster & Glidden, the heating and electrical contractors, wrote in regard to the need to regulate a fan in the Sunday school room, "I propose to order and install that Speed Controller on my own responsibility and leave it to the Church Committee to do whatever they think is right," Ehrman responded with thanks and informed them that "the difference in cost I will take up with you personally sometime later."[5]

While some of these "misunderstandings" and surprise bills were the result of the real need for changes that inevitably occur in the construction process, others were caused by Wrights telling contractors and suppliers to go ahead with changes for which he had not received permission or clearance. This was a practice into which he had fallen early in his career and which he so often got away with that he probably never seriously thought about changing his ways.

He knew that a request for a change order or additional expense might be rejected, and he was always so sure of his own judgment that he tended to go ahead anyway. Also, knowing that he was already so far behind schedule might have contributed to his reluctance to risk slowing down the project even more, alienating both the client and the supplier or contractor. At any rate, the combination of Wright's boldness and confidence and Ehrman's desire for peace and avoidance of confrontation seems like a perfect match for the architect getting his way.

In addition to Wright's propensities, his habits, and his sense of the aesthetic value of his judgments, we can be reasonably certain that his attention to the detail that Ehrman wanted was seriously compromised by the disruptions in his domestic life. Wright had always worked when he wanted, and his appearance at home was always a matter of speculation. However, his recent infatuation with Mamah Cheney and the amount of time he spent away from both his home and the studio to be with her must have exacerbated his already strained schedule. Moreover, though it is only speculation, he may have already considered making a radical break to be with Mamah, and might have been throwing any discretion to the winds, in terms of contracts, payment issues, and related practical aspects of his professional life.

However, we will soon see that there were some limits to what Wright could get away with—at least in regard to the congregation of Unity Temple—and that others were willing to step in where Ehrman feared to tread.

Further finishing took place during the months after the congregation occupied Unity House, with primary attention paid to matters of perfecting the heating and lighting.

The heating was to prove a major concern and then problem, as Wright had planned to have the heat flow from vents in the large piers in the Temple itself, assisted by fans (see fig. 28). However, neither he nor the contractors had really ever experienced such a process and were planning based on square footage, the expectations about the flow of air, and the hope that warmth would reach all sections of the space. We shall see how unfounded those hopes and expectations were.

Major construction included work on the vestibule and Unity Temple itself, and there was even some attention paid to the landscaping around the building. There were constant skirmishes over money, with cost overruns, bills for work for which there was no authorization, and payments exceeding budget.

The congregation was already out of money when called upon to make a $2,500 payment to Paul Mueller by early October, and President Adams informed the board of trustees that he had borrowed that sum from Oak Park Trust and Savings, at 6 percent

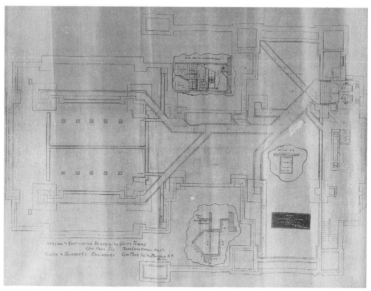

Figure 28. The final plans of the architect indicate the innovative, but dysfunctional, heating system that was to bring warm air through the large hollow piers, as well as the more traditional ways of delivering the other utilities and systems.

interest, in order to make the necessary payment.[6] Further financial complications arose when a certificate for $1,200 was submitted a few weeks later. Not only was the congregation pinched for resources at the time, but the board was very concerned about running ahead of the contract in regard to payments, especially in regard to maintaining the agreed upon reserve. The trustees met in special session on November 11 and debated the matter of payment:

> The sense of the meeting was strongly against payment because of 15% provision in the contract. No definite action was taken, however, but it was left to the Building Committee to investigate the matter further. The meeting then took up in-formally discussion of ways and means for raising money.[7]

Mueller was informed of the board's concern and decision to withhold payment, and he then complained to the architect. Wright contacted President Adams, and he, in turn, wrote to the contractor to further explain the church's position in regard to the contract:

> I told Mr. Wright, as I told you, that the question we were concerned about was whether, if we paid this certificate now there would still be enough money coming to you to complete the contract and pay any unsettled accounts already accrued. Mr. Ehrman and I will look over the statements you left with Mr. Wright, which he says covers these matters, and if we feel that it will be entirely safe to pay this certificate we will take means to get the money together to do so. We were not prepared to be called upon so soon as we have already paid almost 85 per cent of the entire contract price and there is much work left to be done.
>
> I would like to have you send me an affidavit of all unsettled sub-contracts, including any unsettled accounts for labor and materials already purchased, unless a statement to that effect is among those left with Mr. Wright.[8]

Mueller responded by leaving a list of figures with the architect, figures that the president found to be totally unsatisfactory in light of past experience. Yet, reflecting the church's recognition of just how much had already been committed by the contractor, Adams's response—like those of Ehrman—is a blend of economic reality and a desire to be as generous as possible under the circumstances. He was a little tougher than Ehrman, but only a little. His response to Mueller reflects his concerns, his desire not to upset the apple cart, his diplomacy, and the way he appealed to both Mueller and Wright to be scrupulous and honest in return:

> Mr. Ehrman and I have gone over your statements left with Mr. Wright, and have checked them up with the

specifications. We find that you have made no allowance for the pews and the doors or curtains to be placed between the main room and the alcoves and galleries of Unity House. Allowing for these $1,125.00, which is a very conservative figure, and taking the figures of other uncompleted work as estimated by you (which it seems to us are in some instances entirely too low), the account would stand as follows:

Balance on contract, $5,026.15

Extra 645.60

Cost to complete as per your statement $2,950.00

Pews and Doors 1,225.00

———

4,075.00

1,598.75

You will see that this leaves only about $1,600.00 over and above the cost to complete your contract, assuming that it can be done for $4,075.00, which we very much doubt. If we should pay $1,200.00 now, that would leave but $400 to provide for contingencies and any unpaid bills for work or material that has already gone into the building. This leaves too small a margin altogether. Under the contract we are privileged to hold back 15 per cent of the completed work and the entire value of all uncompleted work, which in this case according to your own figures would amount to about $7,500 as against the $5,000, which is all we now owe on the contract. In other words, you have already received $2,000 more than is due under the contract including the bill rendered for extra work.

While I understand as well as any one else that the building is costing you much more than you are going to get out of it, and while for that reason I want to be as liberal in making payments as we can possibly be, yet it is our

duty to see that there is always enough money coming to
you to complete your contract for the price agreed
upon....We have considered the matter very carefully, and
if you will submit evidence that the unpaid bills now due,
and which under the law could ripen into liens on the
building, do not amount to more than $400 or $500, we
will recommend payment of the item for extra excavation
and foundations.[9]

Indeed, it is very interesting that Adams was aware that Mueller
was going to lose money on the job, by this time, and is noting that
everyone else realized it as well. So Mueller could not be fooling
himself into thinking that things would work out all right. It is
doubtful that even Wright could have sweet-talked him into believ-
ing that it would work out by then, but we can only assume that he
had to and wanted to stick with both the job and Wright because
of the prestige of doing this public building and the fact that Wright
had been and still could be a major source of further work.

Additional claims for money were submitted by various subcontractors, from roofers to electricians, and from vendors and the
local utility company; the correspondence of the church is filled
with dunning letters and requests for substantiation for the
remainder of the project. As Foster & Glidden were responsible
for the plumbing and heating and the electrical work, there were
many requests for payment, disagreements as to the amount owed
on individual projects, and continued church protests that submitted bills had not received prior approval. Foster & Glidden also
found their lives and work complicated by the newness of so many
of the processes involved in building Unity Temple, and as was
indicated above in reference to the fan for the Sunday school
room, they often had to return to correct problems that seem not
to have been their fault. In plain fact, there was no way the client,
the architect, the general contractor, or the tradesmen would know
how some of the plans and specifications would work until they

were in place. Paul Mueller had somewhat of a better idea, as he had so much experience working with Wright and, it can be reasonably assumed that Wright gave him oral instructions and discussed issues with him, even if he then went behind his back and made financial commitments that Mueller would have to honor. Nonetheless, some of the more radical innovations had no history behind them, and both Wright and Mueller were flying by the seat of their respective and mutual pants in making things work, let alone in regard to their cost.

Ehrman not only had to negotiate with the various subcontractors and the vendors concerned with, among other items, the pews for the church, but even found himself having to contact a congregant, A. W. Bryant, about the quality of the coal that he was supplying against his financial pledge in support of the new building. Courteous and thorough as always, the building committee chairman noted the size of the clinkers in the furnace and concluded his letter with a specific request for "Pocahontas Coal." When Bryant got somewhat testy in response, suggesting that the congregation check out its equipment and learn how to run a furnace, the ever patient Ehrman carefully and apologetically explained his position in his follow-up letter.[10]

Perhaps because of the lack of financial incentive to do further work at a loss, perhaps because of Mueller's often over-committed and conflicting schedule, the pace of work slowed considerably after November, as evidenced by a comment in a Foster & Glidden letter of January 7, 1908, requesting payment for some of their work:

> We would also like to receive a certificate for a good part of this balance, as our work is practically completed and there does not seem to be anything being done at the church. Therefore, it looks as if it would be next summer, before we could get to finish up the few little odds and end.[11]

What we know of Wright's professional and personal life at this time suggests that he was trying to do way too much. He had used up almost all of the Unity Temple money and was working on houses in Oak Park; Riverside; Madison, Wisconsin; and Buffalo, New York, all of which would bring in much needed funds. Thus, it is hard to imagine his having the time to spend at the site of Unity Temple, making sure things were moving along. Possibly worse, some of the same contractors and workmen may well have been busy at one or more of Wright's other projects. And, as mentioned earlier, there is every indication that Wright was already deeply involved in his romantic relationship with Mamah Cheney, and spending time with her while paying minimal duties at home certainly fragmented his time, his commitments, and his attention.

Yet, work went on—even in a desultory way—through the next few months. Most of the building committee's correspondence through the winter continued in the same vein as the fall, with most of the matters of record concerned with the heating and electrical issues, and with little direct contact with either Wright or Mueller. Perhaps the most interesting letter is the one sent by the Chicago Board of Underwriters, listing some ten items that a recent inspection indicated were deficient in the electrical work payment for which was a constant source of disagreement between the church and Foster & Glidden. The name of H.H. Glidden appears as the manager on the letterhead of the Board of Underwriters, and it is probably fair to assume that he was a relative of the manager of Foster & Glidden, W.W. Glidden.

Though there is no extant record of the conversations between Ehrman and either Wright or Mueller, both the reality of doing business and the written records indicate that both calls and face-to-face meetings often took place. However, only when such a conversation necessitated a follow-up action are we likely to have much insight into matters handled in the less formal manner. From the surviving letters, it is obvious that the church leadership was trying to get major construction underway, again, through the winter and into early spring of 1908, but with little luck. Ed Ehrman must have spoken with Wright about the matter often, and we have specific reference to attempts to break the stalemate, in an exchange of letters between the two men. There were also letters written to Mueller, but the general contractor appears to have been a man of few written words (the church archives containing copies of many letters sent him and very few written responses).

Ehrman referenced one of the conversations with Wright in a letter in which he informed the architect that he had reported their discussion about ways of moving the project along to the board of trustees and that they were awaiting a written proposal and plan from him. He assured him that the board was prepared to pay the bills more frequently but expressed their strong concern that sufficient funds be withheld to guarantee the completion of the building. Wright responded the next day in a characteristically general, genial, and reassuring way:

> In the face of the present financial situation Mr. Mueller, general contractor for your new building, is unable to proceed with your work if he is compelled to leave 15% of the contract price in your hands until the structure is completed.
>
> In view of the fact that he has already put into this structure nearly eleven thousand dollars over and above the sum he is finally to receive from you, when it is completed, I would suggest this technicality be waived and he be paid up closely from time to time, you to retain only such margin as will insure the completion of the building without loss to you. I have no doubt that if this is done the building may be pushed to completion.[12]

The board members were certain of their legal ground both in refusing to make any additional payments until the contractual work had been completed and in maintaining a reserve fund of 15 percent for contingencies, in case of problems that had to be resolved, and to guard against subcontractor demands. Nonetheless—and with extreme trepidation—they concurred with Wright's recommendation and agreed to waive the reserve. Though they had the contract on their side, they were sufficiently men of the world to realize that, with no financial incentive for further work, Mueller could force them into even greater difficulties were they to undertake an expensive and time-consuming legal action. The only course of action consistent with getting Mueller back to work was the one that was going to put some money in his pocket.

The congregation held its annual meeting on Monday, March 30, and, of course, had an update on the construction. As part of the report on the building fund, H.A. Taylor indicated that pledges to the fund were $4,257 shy of the amount necessary to pay all the projected outstanding bills to complete the building. President Adams's call for subscriptions was met with enthusiasm, and within half an hour, the subscription total stood at $5,771. Though subscriptions were not money in the bank, the board of trustees now had sufficient pledges in hand to pay for what it knew would be forthcoming in the way of bills, and an enthusiastic parish membership—at 190 families, its largest ever—felt that they had helped assure the early completion of the building.[13]

With these new commitments in place, all of the outstanding certificates in Mueller's account were settled within a two-week period. As part of what seemed to be a further inducement for Mueller to get to work, he was also offered the opportunity of bidding on yet general plans for newly approved walks and curbs on the grounds.

The incentives seem not to have been compelling, however, for the builder was not quick to respond. Both the president of the board of trustees and the chairman of the building committee wrote to Mueller on April 7, 1908. Adams referenced the letter of March 20, from Wright, and offered to waive the 15 percent requirement if the builder could guarantee that the work could get done within the price agreed upon. He laid out procedures for payment with lien waivers and, with the congregation's recent substantial commitment of financial support in mind, pointed out that the church was now in the position to make prompt payments.[14] Finally, he proposed that he and Ehrman would meet with Mueller to discuss this proposal a few days later and asked him to telephone to set an exact time for the meeting. Ehrman's letter, on the other hand, made no reference to any of this, but simply inquired as to Mueller's interest in costing out the cement and curb work on the grounds. It also asked that the concrete mixer and other equipment be removed if work had been completed on the exterior of the building.[15]

President Adams followed up his letter by phone, and Mueller agreed to the terms outlined. He promised both to accept the proposal, in writing, and to send a statement itemizing the costs of the remaining work needed to complete the project. Another letter from Adams to Mueller, some six weeks later—May 20—refers to that conversation and notes that the board had received nothing in writing to date. He expressed the frustration of the board, pointed out that they did not wish to wait forever, and suggested that unless a written statement confirmed these matters, it could only mean that Mueller did not wish to modify the contract and the 15 percent reserve would be maintained.

We have every indication that Mueller was a man of few words, an even fewer written ones, as there seems to be almost no correspondence in any of the Wright files where letters and memos from everyone else are to be found. It is hard to know if he was just overwhelmed, out of town in Buffalo or elsewhere, or had no incentive to respond to terms that held no additional source of funds for him.

There was still no answer from Mueller, and the patience of even the most dedicated and affable congregants was being tested. With construction still at a standstill, the building committee began receiving complaints about both the appearance of the property and the equipment that remained on and around the grounds. The commissioner of Public Works for the Village of Oak Park wrote and pointed out that Kenilworth Avenue was blocked for close to two years and noted that the village authorities had been quite lenient; nonetheless, he wanted the area cleared.[16] Samuel Packard, an attorney residing across Kenilworth Avenue, also wrote to Ehrman, and his letter (under the letterhead of his law firm) indicates his awareness that construction had ceased some time earlier:

> I have made no complaint heretofore when I understood the contractor was doing his best towards completing the building, although it has been a very great inconvenience to me many times, especially when the contractor worked all night and when the street was so fully occupied that it made it difficult for me to get in and out of my yard with my automobile, and has been a constant eye sore for a long time. It does seem to me now that further patience ceases to be a virtue and that something ought to be done to have the street cleared and the old machinery and debris removed. It is too bad, with such a fine building capable of making the street and locality very attractive, to have this old, dirty repulsive looking machinery and material change the whole effect and destroy the otherwise harmonious surroundings.[17]

A third letter of the same week was written by E. O. Gale, from whom the building lot had been purchased, a man who was an active member of the congregation, and who lived next door to the new building. His letter is brief, to the point, and contains a threat to withhold any further support for the project:

> I am getting pretty well paid out on the confounded condition of the supposed church we were expected to have at some moderate time. The filthy condition of everything on the street and sidewalk pertaining is enough to disgust & has been enough for two years. And I am tired enough to take no more interest in the uncomfortable condition of the present room.[18]

Figure 29. The congregation expected to fully occupy the building by the fall of 1908, and this photograph indicates that almost all of the exterior was complete by the spring of that year. Yet much remained to be done, and work on the basic systems had really only begun. Courtesy Art Institute of Chicago Ryerson/Burnham Library

Given the timing of the letters, one might wonder as to possible collusion, though Ehrman's letters of apology to each suggests that any coordination might have been between the two neighbors and that they, in turn, prompted the inspection by the village authorities. Copies of two of the letters were passed on to Paul Mueller, and as the files contain no further mention of the matter, it appears that a general cleanup must have occurred.

The architect also seems to have been too busy with other projects to respond to the church's requests for action, and Mueller blamed Wright for lack of progress on the pews. Ehrman continued pressuring Wright, writing on July 3 with a request for revised sketches so that Mueller could place a call for bids.

More importantly, nothing was being done on the construction site, and the board of trustees was not only frustrated but also angry that Mueller continued to work on other projects and was ignoring theirs. President Adams, an attorney with the Chicago and Oak Park Elevated Railroad, visited Mueller's office on July 1, but after cooling his heels for half an hour, left without getting to speak with the general contractor. He wrote him later, informing him that he would reappear on the following day, and mentioned that he had been informed by the builder's staff that work was to recommence now that the carpenters had finished their work at the Princess Theatre. Adams further noted, "We have made arrangements for the dedicatory exercises to take place in the early fall and we intend to get the church done in time if we have to do it ourselves."[19] We can safely assume that Adams received no satisfaction on his second visit, either, for the board of trustees passed the following resolution at their monthly meeting on July 5:

> Resolved that the President of the Board be authorized to notify Paul F.P. Mueller, contractor for the church building now being erected by this Society, that unless within five days he proceeds to finish the plastering work in Unity Temple, which has been long delayed, another contractor will be employed to finish said work and the cost thereof charged said Paul F.P. Mueller, as provided by clause 11 of the contract entered into with him on April 28, 1906.[20]

The board seemed to mean business, and Adams followed up with letters to Mueller and C.E. Roberts, the former informed the contractor of the board's action and expressed the hope that they would not be necessary to act on the resolution. In the letter to Roberts, the member of the building committee that Wright recalled with such appreciation, the president noted the need for a certificate from the architect, documenting Mueller's neglect and default. Adams enclosed such a certificate, having prepared it himself, and asked Roberts to have Wright sign it: he wanted it available if needed.[21]

As there is no further direct correspondence about the matter, and as certain steps were taken in regard to the pews and the sidewalks, Mueller must have gotten workmen back on the site over the summer. By the early fall, all of the major construction work was completed, and most of the attention of the board and its committees was concentrated on the final electrical work, the pews, the art glass, and the organ.

Foster & Glidden, the firm that (like Paul Mueller) was actively involved in Frank Lloyd Wright projects both in the Chicago area and Buffalo, New York, had separate contracts for the plumbing and heating and the electrical work, and there were different problems in regard to their two areas of responsibility. The most significant and far reaching, those relating to heating the Temple, had yet to show themselves, and the minor ones, such as the blower problem for the Sunday School area, were usually dispatched with little in the way of technical difficulties. Responsibility and cost remained small but vexing areas of conflict, and we have already noted how Ed Ehrman tended to handle those.

The church had every reason to wish the prompt completion of all remaining work on the building, with a projected dedication for the fall, though much remained to be done. Now, in early August, Foster & Glidden also wished to move quickly, at least in regard to the remaining electrical work. W. W. Glidden, the manager of the firm, wrote Ehrman as follows:

> Our Mr. Clifton is here now, from Buffalo, N.Y. to complete the electrical work on Unity Church.…We have quit the electrical contracting business, and therefore, have no one here to do such work, except when we bring Mr. Clifton back from Buffalo.…Therefore, we shall expect to complete our work within the next four or five days, and we want everything inspected and attended to, in the meantime.[22]

The electrical work was completed during that time, though small problems arose from time to time, and there were disputes about responsibility and payments, in regard to the electrical, plumbing, and—especially—heating work completed by the firm.

As work on the major components of the building, plastering, finishing the walks, the electrical work, and so on neared completion, the board of trustees regained some of their enthusiasm and tried to transmit it to those congregants whose lack of financial support indicated their disbelief in the eventual success of the project. Some congregants had been merely paying interest on their pledges, rather than handing over the cash, and the members of the building committee had to worry about having sufficient funds available to make necessary payments, in addition to their other responsibilities. As usual, Ed Ehrman was responsible, and corresponded with many members about their financial obligations. The overly optimistic leader of the congregation, President Adams, sent a letter to all current subscribers to the building fund, projecting the imminent completion of the building and urging them to pay up:

> Your Trustees are gratified to report that the Church building will be fully completed within the present month, or soon thereafter, and you can readily see the necessity of having sufficient cash in the treasury to make final settlement with the contractors at that time. There is about $9,000.00 yet to be paid on the subscriptions. A portion of this amount has been anticipated by borrowing temporarily at the bank.[23]

The writers pointed out that further borrowing would lead to the added financial burden of additional interest, noted that more than $4,000 in subscriptions were already past due, and averred that if only the delinquent subscriptions were paid, there would be sufficient cash to pay all the outstanding bills *and* to reduce the extant bank debt. The strong pitch concluded on a more realistic note, with the final sentence asking those who could not honor their entire pledge to send whatever they could. The major hurdles seemed to be over, and both the building committee and the board of trustees looked forward to worshiping in a completed building by early fall.

CHAPTER 6

COMPLETING
UNITY TEMPLE

The dedicatory service for the Temple was scheduled for October 11, 1908, and the building committee shifted their attention from bricks and mortar issues to the "art glass" and furnishings for the building. Although making sure that all the glass for the windows and skylights was delivered as designed and ordered required tracking both the architect's changes and the contractor's responses, arranging for the pews and the organ proved to be the most vexing matters at this time.

Church pews have long been a fairly standardized item in church construction, and although the design of Unity Temple was quite unusual, there was never any thought given to seating of an equally radical nature. Indeed, as the original plans and drawings indicated nothing specific about the pews, and Mueller included their cost in his bid, he certainly expected to provide nothing out of the ordinary (fig. 30). This might have been because Wright was being true to the words written about the kind of close, warm place the sanctuary was meant to be, or because the normal pews, in the seating arrangement planned, was both sufficiently like a traditional Unitarian setting, yet suited to the unusual architecture. Yet Wright did have some ideas about finish, color, et cetera, as he always did, whether designing a home, a factory, or a public building.

With no expectation of major issues in mind when the board's plans committee had met in March of 1908, they had recommended only a modified version of one of the standard models sold by a large purveyor of church furniture. With their usual thoroughness, the committee discussed the matter and made detailed suggestions as to the modification of the design of the pew end, the elimination of foot rests, and the substitution of a specially placed book rack for the standardized one that was fairly low on the pew back.[1] Mueller had been sent a copy of both the drawings and the committee's report to the board of trustees, immediately after the latter body approved the design, along with a letter suggesting that he consult Wright and proceed with bids for the pews.[2]

Although there are no records referencing the architect's reaction and response, subsequent letters indicate that he had his own idea of how the pews should look, particularly in regard to their finish, and that the push to have them installed in time for the dedication was carried out equally by letter and telephone. Letters to the American Seating Company (ASC) of Chicago, from President Adams and Chairman Ehrman, both reference unrecorded conversations with Adams and C.E. Roberts, on behalf of the board of trustees, and refer to Mueller's written contract with them and the price of $925. In return, the company refers to Adams's telephone instructions to "finish the furniture for the Unity Church to match in color the sample block which was sent to us by Mr. Mueller, we to put on our regular wax finish in place of the finish as shown on the sample block."[3]

The reason for the calls and multiple letters was the imminence of the dedication of the building, originally scheduled for October 11, 1908. As the contract for the pews had not been awarded until September 8, and was not signed by the president of the board until the 14th, there was real cause for panic. Ed Ehrman wrote the company on the 16th:

Figure 30. While the architect planned only for simple, commercially available pews at the start, and the congregation only modified them by eliminating footrests and changing the placement of the standard bookracks, problems arose in regard to the finish. They were installed days before the first service. Courtesy Unity Temple Restoration Foundation

We understand that you have the order for and are getting seats for Unity Church of Oak Park, from the contractor, Mr. Paul F.P. Mueller. We understand that you are using your best endeavors to get these out promptly, but in behalf of the Building Committee, wish to advise you of the importance to us of the work proceeding without delay. All arrangements have been made for the dedication of the building together with the engagement of a speaker from the East, etc., and our plans will be thoroughly upset if you fail to complete your work in the time arranged for between you and the contractor. You will pardon the seeming intrusion of this committee, but you will appreciate that the whole responsibility to the parish rests upon this committee.[4]

ASC responded to President Adams the next day, informing him that their factory supplier promised delivery by October 6, and admitting that it would be impossible to absolutely guarantee installation by the 11th. They informed the board that they could be certain of completing their work during the following week and returned the contract with a request that the guaranteed date of the 11th be removed. The board agreed to removing the date from the contract, and President Adams then resubmitted the contract to ASC with an expression of hope that the deadline of the 11th would, in fact, be met. As there is no further record of correspondence between the church and ASC until the latter wrote in regard to payment, in mid-December, we can only assume that the pews were delivered sometime in October.

The first service actually conducted in the Temple was eventually held on the 25th of October, though it was not a service of dedication. Indeed, as the dedicatory service did not actually take place for another year and there is no further reference to the October 11 event, the reason for canceling the festivities remains somewhat of a mystery. Perhaps the administration or the minister felt that the building was too far from complete, and from payment, and feared that such a major ceremony would cause the donations necessary to pay the bills to dry up. Other possibilities include the reality that enough details were incomplete as to cause the powers that be to fear that the wrong impression would be given, and that both congregants and the broader public might not understand what remained to be done. Given that subsequent events totally unanticipated in October caused the congregation to vacate the Temple building for some time, the cancellation of the original dedication was to prove fortuitous.

While there seems to have been no problems in regard to the installation of the "art glass" in either Unity House or the Temple, with it all in place by early September of 1908, there is more than a hint that Wright had made unexpected and unauthorized changes while the building was in construction. We have already noted that the architect not only changed his design during the early planning stages, but had also made adjustments during the construction period. As has been recently noted by one Wright biographer, "no design could be called complete until the building itself was complete; to him the process of construction was a process of refinement as well."[5] When the president of the Temple Art Glass Company wrote to President Adams in regard to payments, on October 12, 1908, he not only indicated that all of the glass work was completed, but also indicated the probable changes when he informed Adams that: "All other invoices not stamped paid are for glass ordered by Mr. F.L. Wright, and we must refer you to him to inform you which items are in Mr. Mueller's contract and which are not."[6] Subsequent correspondence between the board, Temple Art Glass, and Wright all focus on finances, with disputes about payment for glass usually bracketed with other similarly disputed items.

Nonetheless, as with so many other matters connected with the erection of the building, Wright seems to have made costly changes during construction, signed certificates in excess of the budgeted

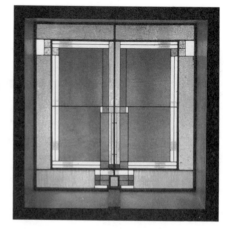

Figure 31. The art glass for Unity Temple is a much-admired part of the building, yet there is almost no discussion of the placement, colors, or design of the wonderful panels in any of the documents relating to the construction. Clearly, the building committee liked what they saw, and few problems arose. Courtesy Unity Temple Restoration Foundation

Figure 32. Other than the subtle aspects of the design of the building, there is no aspect of either the Auditorium or Unity House that more clearly reflects Wright's interest in and the influence of Japanese domestic spaces than in the fixtures that adorn the building. Courtesy Unity Temple Restoration Foundation

amount, and then tried to have the board make payment. Mueller, who was either a poor businessman, was one of the legion of those unable to say no to Wright, or operated in the naïve hope that the congregation would pay without complaining, failed to even attempt to secure board approval for the changes. Thus, when the board confronted Wright with the actual terms of the contract and understandably and justifiably refused to pay for changes they had never approved, Mueller was left holding the bag. As mentioned earlier, this may have been a pattern that had occurred in prior shared projects, but there was apparently something different at work with Unity Temple. Most of the buildings that Wright had completed (and had overages in cost), including the Larkin Building and E-Z Polish, were owned by individuals who could call the shots and respond to changes as they felt. Working with a congregation was different in two regards: first of all, the parish was not a wealthy one, and didn't have large reserves on which to draw. Equally as important, a group of Unitarians and Universalists debated everything, and no one person had the power, authority, or even the disposition, to make unilateral decisions, especially in regard to the expenditure of congregational funds. This itself contributed to some of the delays, as contractors or suppliers who were "ready to roll" one day, might have taken on other responsibilities by the time the committee (and even the congregation) finally agreed to a substantial modification. And in spite of the major issues relating to heating, electrical, etc., there were surprises and additional delays in the most unexpected of quarters.

The design and construction of an organ for the church was an even more vexing and time-consuming project than the pews and stained glass. With at least a dozen firms competing for the privilege of building the organ, there were many more players involved, and the building committee had to face issues relating to its siting, cost, and appearance long before it was constructed, and with repercussions extending long after the completion of the building itself. In fact, the ashes of the original church building were barely cold before the congregation was approached by the first of what came to be a very determined group of representatives of the various companies that were engaged in the building of pipe organs.

Emmons Howard, the president of the company of the same name, wrote the minister on June 21, 1905, just a couple of weeks after the June 4 conflagration, as follows: "We are advised that you are about to erect a new church edifice and presume that upon its completion you will require a pipe organ for same."[7] As was apparently industry practice at that time, he went on to suggest that if the dimensions of both the room and the space allowed for the organ were provided, he would be happy to provide specifications and bid on the project. The writer never referred to the fire nor expressed his regrets at the destruction of their church, leaving us in doubt as to whether he actually was aware that the church had been destroyed or if his source of information had only conveyed the congregation's approval of the concept at their May meeting. The other firms that similarly approached the congregation also wrote directly to the minister, most likely as it would be difficult to know whom to approach otherwise, while the clergyman's name would be readily obtainable from various directories. Many of the purveyors offered to make a visit to the site, and almost all either provided the names of Chicago area churches for whom they had already provided organs or suggested the availability of appropriate references.[8] Several of the organ companies were quite persistent, writing every few months and asking if the "organ matter had been taken up yet," and each pointed out that construction took some time. Some mentioned having backlogs of up to six months, and all advised an early contract so that the organ would be ready when needed. Most of the firms offered to have a representative visit with the building committee or the organist personally, and some sent postage-paid envelopes or postcards to assure a response.

Ehrman kept putting these solicitors off until the Temple was sufficiently advanced to move the organ up on the list of priorities. He wrote to Wright on May 22, 1907, mentioning that it took time to get an organ built and asked the architect for a "detail plan of the space available for the pipe organ."[9] He noted that a pencil drawing would be sufficient but also asked that the dimensions be written in to avoid errors. There is no record of a response, but the fact that at least one of the prospective builders referenced the sketches he saw in Wright's office that July seems to document the fact that he complied fairly, and unusually, quickly.

The organ builders' responses to the space were uniformly negative: Lyon & Healy of Chicago examined the drawings and blueprints in Wright's office and wrote Ehrman, "It appears that a space 8′ deep and with ample width has been provided for the organ. The height for the most part is not more than 6′ or 7′ with a very small portion of the chamber running up to 20′. The chamber as it is is of no value to the organ builder."[10] The writer noted that he would have been happy to offer practical advice and suggested a meeting with both the architect and Ehrman himself, the clear implication being that he believed that the church representative would see his point and override the architect's impractical plans. Wright seems to have had no idea of changing his design, and the correspondence of the next several months is a study in both frustration on the part of Lyon & Healy and the all-but-endless patience and optimism of Ed Ehrman.

The latter wrote to Lyon & Healy on July 26, 1907, stating, "Immediately upon the receipt of your letter I had a talk with Mr. Wright in which I think I set matters straight. He has probably written you before this time, but should you not hear from him within a few days, I would esteem it a kindness if you would so advise me by phone."[11] The organ builders responded on August 15, noting that they had yet to hear from Wright. There were several subsequent letters and calls, with Ehrman writing the architect on October 2:

> I have correspondence under the following dates,—July 13th, July 19th, August 15th, & August 16th concerning appointments and this has been supplemented by at least two 'phone messages to you by myself, but so far without success. Will you not make a special effort to put yourself into communication with Mr. Wells immediately so that he may make an effective appointment with you? Your promptness in attending to this matter will be appreciated by him as well as by the building committee.[12]

Wright would not let himself be budged on this matter, no doubt because changing the space would have upset his spatial conception and the relationship of the modules, and a Lyon & Healy letter of November 5 clearly underscores the different agendas of the architect and several of the organ builders. They referenced the inadequate space permitted by the architect and declined to bid for the privilege of building the organ.

The building committee understood the problem associated with the space for the organ, but the evidence is that they favored urging the prospective organ builders to see what they were up against before submitting any bids.[13] By the fall of 1907, Ehrman was communicating with a dozen firms engaged in building organs, informing them:

> [T]he fact that the space allotted the organ by the architect is rather irregular would make it necessary for your representative to see the building in order to intelligently make an estimate. Am mailing you a B.P. showing the space available. The building, however, is unusual in design and I doubt if the B.P. will give you much of an idea unless aided by a personal visit.[14]

Because of the special nature of an organ purchase, the instrument being essentially built to order both to the stated needs of the client and the acoustics of the particular space, it was not at all unusual for those contemplating such a purchase to employ a consultant. Given the design issues raised in Ehrman's letter, the trustees of Unity Church felt that such a consultant would aid them in their negotiations with the representatives of the various organ building companies, and Charles F. Rowe was retained for that purpose. Thus, when Hillgreen, Lane, & Co., of Alliance, Ohio, wrote to the pastor to solicit the commission for the organ they understood to be contemplated, they were sent a copy of Wright's drawings and dimensions, along with the news that they ought to make their presentation directly to Mr. Rowe. In separate responses to the minister, to the head of the building committee, and to Rowe, they conveyed a great deal of information about the process, their fears, and their sense of the need for diplomacy. They asked Rowe to contact them when he completed his specifications and details of construction, and expressed the hope that he would examine some of the organs already built in the Chicago area. They informed the chairman of the building committee of their contact with the consultant and the minister, and they mentioned their current organ construction for the Congregational Church in nearby Austin to all

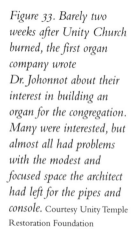

Figure 33. Barely two weeks after Unity Church burned, the first organ company wrote Dr. Johonnot about their interest in building an organ for the congregation. Many were interested, but almost all had problems with the modest and focused space the architect had left for the pipes and console. Courtesy Unity Temple Restoration Foundation

three correspondents. They saved the most delicate points for Dr. Johonnot, however: "From other sources, we have heard of the character of the structure," and from the same letter:

> We confess, however, to an inability to clearly understand the drawings sent us, though we have consulted with other Architects of our city. The drawings of the elevation are especially puzzling, though the floor plan indicates a room of ample area. Of course we have not reported to the Architect the trouble we have experienced in interpreting his drawings.[15]

Ehrman was concerned about the issue, but still hoped that something could be worked out without a confrontation, so he wrote to Rowe:

> There certainly is no harm whatever in your conferring with him [Wright] personally, or Mr. Lane conferring with him personally at any time either of you see fit. The point I wish to bring out is, that it is a little too early at the present time to try to *officially* settle the matter above referred to—that of the available organ space–vs–necessary organ space.[16]

Not all of the prospective bidders were put off by the reality of the space, and some asked for very minor modifications to accommodate standard equipment. The range of response was from that of Lyon & Healy, whom we noted chose not to even bid on the project; firms such as the Estey Organ Company were to suggest that the space for the organ would have to be made somewhat wider if they were to bid at all; J.W. Steere and Son were to plead for a little more room; while M.P. Moeller was the most accommodating and flattering to the consultant, stating that "although the space and position is somewhat different than usually, I think that it is very practical and I will say that Mr. Rowe is very competent in planning organs."[17]

There was much technical consultation as well, and Rowe was able to negotiate with the various bidders on matters as diverse as the number of pipes, cabinetry, blowers, etc. By early spring of 1908, Ehrman felt he was in a position to narrow down the number of bidders and, as a courtesy, contacted the architect about his preferences. In response to Ehrman's letter of March 19 and his call on the 20th, Isabel Roberts, Wright's valued secretary, wrote to tell the building committee chairman that among all the competing firms, he liked Lyon & Healy and the Erie Organ Co. best, and favored the proposal and plans submitted by the latter.[18]

Meanwhile, the ever-industrious Ehrman not only met with the representatives of several of the firms, discussing the plans and trying to get them to lower the price, if possible, but also did his own financial check on each company's financial standing. An undated handwritten sheet probably also prepared that spring, and on the letterhead of Walker & Ehrman Mfg. Co., lists seven of the firms, their financial rating by R.G. Dunn & Co., and his evaluation of their standing.[19] Kimball and Lyon & Healy had the highest rating of Triple A, but each was to withdraw from the competition before the church was even close to making a decision on the organ.

Each of the companies still pursuing the matter wrote just about monthly, through the summer of 1908, each apologizing for nagging, yet fearing lest they appear uninterested in securing the contract. When Ehrman returned from his annual vacation in early September, he wrote all those who had contacted him over the preceding several weeks, informing them that "the matter is in a somewhat unsettled condition," and promising to let them know when things moved toward a resolution. Surprisingly, Ehrman was not telling the supplicants all he knew, considering both his usual painstaking directness and the manner in which he had referred all comers to Rowe at an earlier date.

Somewhere between December of 1907 and the summer of 1908, Rowe disappeared from the scene and was replaced by a Mr. Hemington, who seems to have been hired as a new consultant for the church and to supervise the installation of the organ. Coburn & Taylor, one of the Chicago-based organ companies, and the surprise winner of the contract, wrote him at the end of August in regard to their specifications for a twenty-stop organ, beginning their letter with, "We are informed that you are to be asked to look over and pass upon a specification…that we have prepared for Unity Church."[20] Thus, when Ehrman wrote to the remaining bidders in September without mention of Hemington, he seems to have at least been privy to a plan to let Coburn & Taylor attempt

to come to terms with the church without giving the other bidders an equal chance. It is impossible to trace that decision, for neither the minutes of the board of trustees nor the voluminous
correspondence of the building committee makes any reference to
the matter of the organ until the contract with Coburn & Taylor
was drawn up late in September. Indeed, the only other communications between Ehrman and anyone outside the congregation at
that time were in regard to the position of organist, and those soliciting such a position were referred to C.S. Woodward, chairman of
the music committee.

Then, on October 26, 1908, Ehrman wrote as follows to those
who had again contacted him since the round of correspondence
in September:

> The writer found your letter of the 10th instant on his
> desk on his return and begs to state that the organ matter
> was referred to a committee who engaged the services of
> an expert, and acting on his recommendation have placed
> an order for the organ. In closing our correspondence on
> this subject the writer begs to thank you for the courte-
> sies extended to him while making inquiries and seeking
> information.[21]

Though, again, this letter gives no indication of the fact that
Hemington had been hired prior to the previous written interchange (nor why Coburn & Taylor had been awarded such an
advantage), Ehrman belatedly informed the other competitors that
an outside expert had entered the picture and that he was responsible for the decision that the committee had already ratified.

A contract was signed on September 23, 1908, with Coburn &
Taylor agreeing to complete and install the organ, at a cost of
$3,500 (up $500 from the original price budgeted by the board), in
the space of only two months instead of the four to six suggested
by most of the other companies.[22] Perhaps the short construction

time promised by this firm and their proximity in Chicago were sufficiently important considerations in granting them the contract without last-minute competition. The payment plan was liberal, calling for $1,000 upon completion of the instrument and quarterly payments of $500 over the following fifteen months.

There are neither references to the organ, nor correspondence with Coburn & Taylor until after the organ was completed in February of 1909, and then it was in the form of a letter from the company requesting that the church begin paying for the instrument. Thereafter, and for the next three years, there is frequent correspondence between Ehrman—later in his new role as chairman of the organ committee—and Coburn—now on his own as Coburn Organ Co., with the same telephone number, and just down the street from the original partners' office—about continued kinks in and problems with the instrument. Hemington is still referenced and involved in these negotiations as late as April 1912, when Ehrman wrote and summarized his most recent correspondence with Coburn.[23] By that date the troubles seem to have been reduced to sluggishness in the "action," and as there is no further record of interaction between the church and Coburn, it seems safe to conclude that the remaining problem was resolved to the congregation's satisfaction.

During the weeks and months after the aborted dedication of the building and during the time the organ was under construction, several unanticipated issues occupied the time and attention of the members of the building committee. Some were matters relating to performance on work contracted for; some continued to be disputes about payments regarding additional work or modified specifications. However, a problem unique in the process of completing the building arose in regard to a series of planters Wright designed for the Temple but which were never approved in the plans as finally accepted by the church board.

The original interior section drawings for the sanctuary indicate at least six large planters in place on both sides of each section of the

Figure 34. At least six planters appear in the original drawings of the sanctuary. The planters later were rejected by the board, even after they were delivered to the work site.

lower balcony and two atop the piers on the sides of the pulpit (fig. 34); it is probably safe to assume that the remaining two would have been found on the sides of the lower balcony on the north side, the one cut away in the section. Thus, the building committee was not encountering one of Wright's changes in midstream; the planters were part of his plan all along. The available records contain no written reference to the planters during the time the plans were under discussion, so there is no certain way to determine whether they were removed from the proposal at an early date or if they had merely been viewed as a decorative part of the drawing and had never been discussed at all. The written evidence—the correspondence between President Adams and the person who had fabricated the urns, a Mr. Gensch, and even Adams's references to Wright—seems to indicate that the urns were a complete surprise rather than the reintroduction of an expense that had been previously dismissed. Adams wrote to Gensch on Tuesday, October 20, as follows:

> We were informed for the first time on Sunday, October 18, 1908, that you had made and were about to deliver 8 large cement vases to be installed in our new Church building in Oak Park. This work was done entirely without our knowledge or consent, and I take the first opportunity to

advise you that we refuse to accept these vases or to be responsible for the cost thereof, and you are notified not to instal said vases in the Church, nor to deliver them upon our property.

I am going to take the matter up with Mr. Wright, the architect, and I would request that you do no further work on these vases until I have seen him, and can lay the whole matter before our board of trustees, which is the only body that can bind the Church to accept and pay for this work.[24]

Adams immediately visited the architect, and he was reassured that the board had no financial liability for the planters in dispute. We can also imagine Wright making a plea for the inclusion of the planters, being convinced of their aesthetic contribution to the overall effect he desired. Perhaps he even intimated that he would pay for them himself to assure their inclusion. More than likely, he hoped that the church would agree with his taste once the urns were in place and would then agree to pay for them. Judging from the available drawing, the planters were similar to those Wright had already been placing on such homes as the Dana House (1902) and was to continue to so place for the remainder of his years in Oak Park.[25] However, as the board found reason to disagree with the architect, we have no way of knowing the impact they would have actually made.

President Adams called Gensch the morning after he had written, and as soon as he had visited with Wright, to inform the contractor that the church was neither required nor willing to pay for the planters and to inquire as to their current status. Gensch told Adams that he and Wright had agreed to have him deliver them that very day, and that they were already on their way to Oak Park. Adams was justifiably concerned about having to assume responsibility for the work on the planters and, after finding that the price of the planters came to $250, informed Gensch that the only way he could permit him to deliver the pieces was with the understanding that Wright, not the church, would have to pay. Gensch "then said that he would look to Mr. Wright alone for payment of the bill and would install them in the Church on that understanding."[26] Adams opined that he would rather talk it all over after seeing the planters in person and asked Gensch to meet him at the site at 5:00 P.M. that day. He further suggested that the planters could be left on the east patio if the wagons had to leave before he arrived. Finally, he called Ehrman with a request to join him at the site and the latter agreed to also get Roberts to join them.

The wagon that was delivering the planters broke down and never appeared that day, and when Adams tried to reach the contractor, he could not be located. When the wagon finally arrived on the following day, Charles Roberts was the trustee in attendance, and he tried to stop the men from unloading the truck. They, however, cited Adams's approval to leave them at the east entrance and insisted on so doing. After all of the involved board members had a look at the planters late on the 22nd, Adams wrote one final letter to Gensch, explaining the Church's position, asserting its authority over the architect, and ending the affair:

> After looking at these works of art whatever doubts we had as to the advisability of installing them were quickly dispelled and we would not put them in the Church at any price. They would not only hide and obstruct the view of at least forty persons (and every particle of the seating capacity of the Church must be available as it now falls far below what we were assured of) but would overhang the balcony pews and the steps leading to the balconies to such an extent as to materially and seriously interfere with the head room. They are absolutely impractical and must be taken away at once.[27]

As the above referenced drawing of the church interior illustrates Adams concerns exactly, we can probably accept it as fact that the church leaders were totally unprepared for the inclusion of the planters rather than just concerned about the cost implications. If they had seen the drawing, they would have already known that the views would have been compromised. And, given Adams's emphasis on the problem of insufficient seating, we can see that the capacity of the sanctuary was already a sore point with the board of trustees.

In spite of Adams's clear attempt to head off the delivery of the planters and the fact that he did everything possible to reach Gensch before they arrived, he, like Ehrman, was very much a gentleman and extended himself to minimize the impact of the rejection on Gensch. Adams concluded his letter to the contractor with, "I feel that I was at fault in allowing you to leave them upon our property under any consideration, and in view of that fact I will, after they have been taken away, send you my personal check for $25.00 to defray the expense of moving them."[28] As there is no further reference to the planters, we can assume that Gensch removed them without additional fuss, and that Adams followed through with his check.

As discussed, there were ongoing issues relating to the completion of the new church from late autumn of 1908 to January of 1909, in particular, problems relating to the pews, art glass, and the organ. Ehrman, as chairman of the building committee, had attended to all of them while President Adams, for some unknown reason, chose to handle the matter of the planters. Ehrman's biggest problem, and the one of most consequence to the congregation, was the failure of the heating system to adequately warm the building. The matter was quite complicated, involving not only the question of the appropriateness of the system called for by the architect, but also questions of human error, financial responsibility, and the need for emergency measures. The congregation could wait if the organ were not ready on time, it could function without pews until they appeared, and could survive any number of minor deficiencies while they were being resolved, but they could not function in an unheated building in the middle of a Chicago winter. A serious problem called for a prompt and equally drastic solution, and Ehrman was to spend the greatest part of the large amount of time he devoted to the church in working with the architect, two contractors, and several other players in resolving the manner in which the building could be heated.

Wright's design called for an unusual and innovative solution to heating the new building, by having a steam boiler warm air that would be carried through the massive yet hollow columns of the building, rather than one of the more conventional types of radiation or venting systems. The local firm of Foster & Glidden agreed to build it to the specifications and guarantee a "temperature of 70 degrees in weather 10 below zero."[29] There seemed to be no doubt about the feasibility of such a system, with no record of discussions about the heating system until it was installed, and with none of the wrangling that had accompanied other aspects of the design as reported above. However, when the weather turned cold soon after the first service was conducted in the Temple on October 25, 1908, it was discovered that no matter how high the boiler was pushed, it proved impossible to reach that temperature, and the church could not be made to stay warm enough for the congregation. In addition, much of the heat that was generated by the system apparently leached out through the still uncured concrete walls of the building.[30]

The inadequacy of the heating system became evident within a month of the supposed completion of the interior of the Temple. Ed Ehrman started what was to be a lengthy and complicated correspondence with Foster & Glidden in regard to the problem. It was also a correspondence distinguished by unusual bluntness on both sides of the issue, with a clear assumption of the guilt of the other party on both sides, and by Ehrman making demands and accusations out of character when compared to his dealings with others with whom he failed to see eye to eye. When we consider how carefully he seems to have always chosen his words, and when we recall the patience he exhibited in his dealings with Wright,

Mueller, and others, the tone of his letters to the heating contractors makes it clear that he must have felt very much put upon.

There were obviously some calls in which Ehrman tried to impress the contractor with the need for prompt action, for his first written communication asks what progress is being made to "fulfill the requirements of our contract with you," as well as referencing the congregation's helplessness and notes that "you cannot expect us to be satisfied with other than prompt and energetic action on your part in putting your heating system in proper condition of satisfactory service."[31] W.W. Glidden responded with an apology that work had not started earlier and an explanation that the worker who was to install the radiator pipes (a solution to the problem apparently arrived at some days earlier) was incapacitated by rheumatism and that his other people were tied up in other jobs. He promised to get at the work very soon, and promised to have his people work ten hour days until the job was done. He also opined that the matter was not entirely the fault of his company, pointing to the extra expense and inconvenience they had incurred because of the delays before the building was sufficiently completed to the point that they could even begin their work on the plumbing and heating.

In another letter written on the same day, Glidden outlined the steps his company was prepared to take in an attempt to rectify the problem with the heating, having already conferred with C.E. Roberts, the member of the building committee who was an engineer by profession and to whom both President Adams and Ed Ehrman turned for advice on many of the more technical aspects of the construction project:

> We propose to install 800 or 900 feet of 1¼" Pipe coil on the ceiling of the Basement of the Auditorium. We propose to install 800 sq ft of Cast Iron radiation 44" high in the Foyer along the wall between the steps leading from the Foyer to the auditorium. The same to be connected to

the heating system under Unity House all work to be done in neat and workman like manner.

We are to furnish all Labor for the same and the cast Iron radiation, You to pay for the Pipe and fittings. This we propose to do Because in the estimation of the Committee and the heating Contractor it will be necessary to keep heat in Unity Temple practically all the time in order to get satisfactory results. And it is understood that Foster & Glidden are not to be held responsible for the results if the radiation shall be boxed as the Architect Suggests.[32]

Ehrman responded with an undated but obviously prompt letter in which he urges all possible haste in completing the job and expressing his concern that the radiation was not yet available. Moreover, he noted that: "You mention nothing in your outline of proposed alterations and additions about any further corrections in the hot air system, either in the matter of additional boiler capacity or additional air inlets," and warned that they should also be modified if that were required in order to bring the system up to the level of productivity called for in the contract.[33]

The auxiliary radiator system was not installed for several weeks, and the congregation found it necessary to vacate the Temple and once again return to Unity House for Sunday services, starting on December 6, 1908. The bursting of the boiler sometime late in December or early in January further complicated the picture, demonstrating the inadequacy of the system, yet with each party denying responsibility. The parish claimed that the contractor had installed an inadequate system, while Foster & Glidden blamed the church for failing to handle and supervise the system in an appropriate manner. Eventually, the contractor agreed that they should have installed a boiler of larger capacity, and agreed to share the cost of a larger one and swallow the installation and connection fees. They refused to yield on the broader issue of the adequacy of the heating plant itself, and a stalemate was reached by mid-January.[34] Foster & Glidden submitted their final bill for the additional work, on February 27, 1909, but the ongoing disputes about the locus of the responsibility for the inadequacy of the system caused the church to reject it for more than half a year.

Due to the critical situation of a Chicago winter with no heat in the building, the congregation felt that they had to act to replace the boiler and then worry about the responsibility for the accident later. Thus, President Adams contacted Wright about a proposed course of action, as follows:

> It is for obvious reasons out of the question to delay installing a new boiler until we have settled possible differences with the Foster & Glidden Company and in view of our rather disastrous experiences with them in the past and the further fact that they have never shown the ability to exercise that degree of promptness which the present situation imperatively demands, we have made arrangements with another contractor to furnish and instal a new boiler. We would like to have you notify the Foster & Glidden Company of this fact and further that we do not intend to waive any rights we may have against them in case it develops either that they were responsible for the bursting of the boiler or that the system they have furnished does not comply with their contract or fulfil the guaranties therein contained.[35]

Adams was an attorney employed by the Chicago and Oak Park Elevated Railroad Company, and his concern for a clear paper trail was manifest in the way he pursued this matter. He wrote to Wright again, the very next day, asking if he had already been in contact with Foster & Glidden, and noting, "It is very important from a legal standpoint that they be notified of the decision of the Board as outlined in my letter to you at once."[36] The architect acted unusually promptly, speaking for himself instead of conveying the wording of the president, and Isabel Roberts sent Adams a copy of his communication the next morning. Wright gave the contractor three days to remedy the problem "in a manner satisfactory to the architect," with the threat that "Unity Church will enter upon the work and make such additions and changes as are necessary," and concluding, "The cost of so doing shall be charged to your contract."[37] Whether in the interest of brevity or to avoid a conflict, he failed to mention that the building committee had already decided to bring in another contractor.

Glidden answered immediately, referring to all the additional radiation already installed in the auditorium and explaining that he had already contacted Ehrman about the cost of the repair or replace alternatives on the 18th. He stated that he had been waiting to hear from the church as to whether they were going to repair the boiler or reach an agreement with his firm about the repair or replacement before determining what additional steps needed to be taken to bring the system up to par. He also laid the blame for the boiler explosion more squarely on the janitor at the church than had been the case in prior correspondence, and denied any responsibility for the consequent damage. Finally, he informed Wright, "we hereby notify you, as Architect, that any work, changes, or alterations, or additions made to the Heating plant in the said Unity Church, by you, or the church committee, is done at your own risk and expense."[38]

Adams was neither happy with Wright's letter to Glidden nor with the latter's response. He wrote the contractor himself, this time, and enclosed a copy of his request that Wright contact them about the building committee's intent to bring in another contractor to replace the boiler. He then carefully and specifically enumerated the outstanding issues, from the church's point of view: after a new boiler was installed, they would test the entire system and determine if it fulfilled Foster & Glidden's obligation under the contract; the fault for the loss of the original boiler was still under investigation, and the church was not about to conclude that

Foster & Glidden were blameless; that another contractor had been hired to replace the boiler, and that the church waived none of its rights to secure financial relief in regard to any of these matters.[39] Glidden responded with self-righteous indignation:

> In reply, please allow us to say we believe that you have exceeded your right, either legal or moral in putting another contractor on the Unity Church job. Foster & Glidden Co. have made every effort to complete their work promptly, and save in the case of delay in the delivery of radiation, have pushed our work fast as any one would or could under the circumstances; therefore, we shall absolutely refuse to be responsible for any changes, additions or alterations that you may make to that plant.[40]

He also stated that the heating plant had several minor imperfections that his firm had intended to address, and noted that they were unable to complete their work due to the boiler explosion. He concluded with a reiteration of their unwillingness to either share the responsibility or the cost of work done by another contractor.

Although we can easily understand the congregation's concern and even its annoyance at this point in the project, the trustee's position and response seem inconsistent when compared to those taken in regard to other problems that had arisen in the preceding several years. Also, Foster & Glidden seem to have been held accountable for the possible inadequacy of the heating system Wright designed for the building. It seems they also were blamed for the delays that made it impossible to test the equipment before the onset of winter created an emergency when the system proved incapable of maintaining the temperature as per contract. Reviewing the correspondence, it appears with our hindsight that the church would have been in a much stronger position by allowing Foster & Glidden to repair the boiler and make its tests before bringing a third party onto the scene. And as the available record presents the architect as little more than the mouthpiece for the board's actions, we have no idea how Wright felt about the matter. Even if he had minimal interest in these problems when the building was near completion, the fact that he had frequent involvement with Foster & Glidden—both in Oak Park and, as we have seen, Buffalo—would seem to suggest that he would take the same kind of role as peacemaker that he continued to take in the ongoing financial disputes between the church and Paul Mueller.

For whatever reason, the board of trustees had clearly lost faith in Foster & Glidden and, ignoring Glidden's protestations, allowed their newly hired Chicago plumbing and heating contractor, William Lees, to install a new boiler. Less than a week after Glidden wrote to Adams protesting the church's contemplated action, Ehrman informed them that a new boiler had been installed and called upon the contractors to check out the entire system immediately. In a handwritten note dated Saturday, January 30, he asked that they conduct the tests on the following Monday and Tuesday, with the church's building superintendent on hand to operate the boiler and fans at their direction. He dismissed the points made by Glidden in regard to unfinished items as either irrelevant, mooted by the installation of the new boiler, or matters to be corrected at a later date, and concluded that the church would "brook no further delay on your part to satisfy yourselves, as well as ourselves, as to the capacity of the system to do the work. If you have not made the trial by Tuesday evening we shall undertake to do it ourselves."[41]

In spite of the unresolved issues and the lost opportunities for compromise, the tests did go ahead as demanded by Ehrman. They began at 9:30 A.M. on February 1, 1909, and continued, every hour on the half hour, through 4:00 P.M. on the 2nd. Mr. Hammond, the congregation's building superintendent, varied the steam pressure at the direction of Foster & Glidden. At the end of the two days, the temperature had slowly risen from 32 to a final reading of 65 degrees: the contracted temperature of 70 degrees was never reached.[42] Though the results of the test were unsatisfactory, and the Auditorium could not be heated to the desired temperature, the congregation resumed services in the Temple itself on Sunday, February 14, 1909.

Desperate to find a solution to the ongoing problem of an inadequately heated building, the building committee again turned to William Lees, and he installed additional direct radiation to the Auditorium. He completed his work early in March, but warned the congregation, "I do not want you to think the plant is in a first class and safe condition."[43] He enumerated several problems: 1,800 feet of radiation with supply and return pipes that were two small for the job; the need for additional direct radiation in Unity House and a separate feeder and return line thereto; the need to remove the oil from the boiler and the piping. He also was prophetic in pointing out the desirability of installing the larger pipes in the Auditorium "to pitch the proper way so they will circulate in a noiseless manner."[44] And although the record is not clear, he may have also bypassed the warm air system completely, at the same time. The board of trustees very much appreciated his work, and in an unusually prompt manner, Ehrman forwarded a check for two-thirds of his bill of $751.42 the day he received the above report.[45] In spite of finding themselves deeper in debt for the additional work, the trustees apparently decided to add the additional radiators in Unity House, and Lees completed that work in the next two weeks. His final activity at the church occurred when Ehrman wrote to ask him to have the radiators painted to match the walls behind them in time for the building's dedication in September.[46]

CHAPTER 7

DISASTER TO DEDICATION

With the construction of the organ, the installation of the pews and the art glass, and the repair and additions to the heating system, Unity Temple was moving toward completion, in the Spring of 1909. Much of the final burst of activity lay in the realm of finances. Some of the outstanding bills were for work necessarily completed at the end of the project, such as those for the final plastering and painting of the Auditorium and for the heating additions discussed above. Others, like the disputed charges for art glass above the amount in the original contract, had dragged on for a year or more. As had been the case a year earlier, when Wright persuaded the church both to pay Mueller more rapidly than stipulated by the contract and to waive their right to withhold 15 percent until the job was completed, a similar set of multiple negotiations took place between the church, Wright, Mueller, and the affected contractors. And, as had been the case in the previous round of negotiations, the congregation was out of money. The differences were that: with the building essentially complete, the board had little reason to compromise; Mueller's reserve having been eroded, they were left with no cushion at all; and with the bills pretty much all in, they could see how much over budget they had gone.

Wright was of limited help to Mueller this time because the board's president, Adams, was more apt to believe that the work had been completed, to deny congregational responsibility for non-budgeted items, and to tell Wright to divide up the remaining funds among the creditors. With the board of trustees taking a harder line than they had the previous year and more willing to leave unpaid some of the disputed bills for work already completed, Wright no longer had any leverage, nor was he in the position to argue Mueller's case for work that, indeed, never had been approved. In fact, as the architect probably would have been responsible for authorizing most or all of the extra work, and seeing the mood of the board of trustees, he must have realized that to volunteer that he had suggested changes or additions would have certainly led the board to inform him that those bills were then his responsibility. Indeed, he was to go so far as to point out in response to a letter from President Adams that he had not issued certain certificates, "I think there is no further occasion for holding up certificates. As a matter of fact no one has suggested doing so except myself."[1] He also mentioned a lien placed by McNulty and said that he had issued a completion certificate to stop him from putting a lien on the property. He added, almost as an aside, "You are welcome to hold him off longer if you can. If you have written him that there is not enough left to pay him you have probably precipitated his lien."[2]

After the round of correspondence in early March of 1909, the board had no further written communications about the responsibility for the outstanding bills. Whether because of additions, changes, or the inclusion of work neither noted in the signed contract nor approved by the board in writing, they claimed that all were the responsibility of someone else. For all practical purposes, the board was telling contractors with whom they had no dispute about the quality of the work to seek satisfaction from Mueller; they were telling those few with whom there was still a dispute about meeting the terms of the contract, like Foster & Glidden, to absorb their own mistakes; they were telling Mueller (usually through Wright) that it was his own fault for running over the contracted amount and that he could expect no further relief from them. Thus, the bills from Foster & Glidden, from the painting contractor, T.C. Gleich, and, most of all, Mueller, remained as open questions after the building was completed. Although there were several examples of the kind of interchanges between Adams and Wright, Adams's response to the letter of March 8, just cited, is typical. He wrote the architect, on the 12th: "I notice that you also state that Mr. Mueller is entitled to compensation for extra work but that the amount which he claims therefor has not yet been given you. We do not know of any extra items that Mr. Mueller is entitled to, and we wish also to call your attention to the fact that we have paid out some moneys which we claim are chargeable to Mr. Mueller, particulars of which I gave you in my letter dated January 18th last. We wish to be fully heard before any amount is certified by you as due Mr. Mueller for extra work."[3]

Most of the negotiations took place in March and April, with both Ehrman and Adams involved in the correspondence with the other principals. Ehrman attempted to work directly with the individual contractors, resolving unanswered questions and making sure that each project was completed to satisfaction. Adams negotiated matters of fiscal responsibility and alterations in the contract to resolve current and threatened liens on the building. The treasurer, J.H. Heald, then paid the bills as directed by Ehrman. As throughout the project, Mueller's activities are documented by reference in the letters between members of the board of trustees and Wright; the supervising contractor continued to put neither his concerns nor his own interpretation of the figures on paper.[4] Some of the payments were only made after Mueller agreed to credit them to his account, at a time when the congregation no longer believed that it owed him anything at all. Given the lack of a more detailed paper trail, we cannot know whether or not Mueller ever expected to be reimbursed for those expenditures, and there is no further

Figure 35. The interior of Unity Temple has remained remarkably unchanged from its appearance in this early photograph. The strong geometrical organization of the building is striking, with walls, ceiling lighted areas, the speakers platform, and even our views into the lower areas all emphatically divided into cubes, squares, and rectangles.

correspondence with the architect about the matter of dispersal of funds. The subcontractors who were directed to Mueller found him to be no source of money whatsoever, and they were to return to the board for satisfaction in the future.

Most—but not all—of the final amounts due, and for which the congregation felt the need to pay were resolved in early April, and there were a flurry of letters and payments on April 3, 1909, to the hardware supplier, the plasterer, and the painter, but most definitely not including Foster & Glidden. Adams sent a letter to each, noting that he was enclosing a check for the balance of what was owed and asking for a receipt. In the case of McNulty, he said that the check would be delivered upon the release of the lien placed on the property of the church. The release was given the same day, April 3.

The annual meeting of the parish was held, as per the by-laws, in March of 1909. There, Wright's strong supporter and patron, C.E. Roberts, after Ehrman the most active member of the building committee, was elected president. Reverend Johonnot outlined the events of the year to the crowd assembled in the Auditorium. He reviewed the progress toward the completion of the building, over the past year, and pointing out that, at that time, the Temple itself had not been plastered, the connecting vestibule was not ready for use, and that services were being held in Unity House with the back door being used as the only door. He also discussed the disaster of the heating system, how the Temple itself had been opened for worship on October 25 and the return to Unity House in December due to the inadequacy of the heat in the space. He explained the accident to the boiler and the steps taken to get adequate heat in the sanctuary.

The parish membership had climbed back to 140, and the financial condition of the church was discussed. During the last two weeks of March, the members of the board of trustees, including those—like Ehrman—who also served as members of the ad hoc subscription committee, contacted individual church members about the annual deficit of approximately $500, asking for pledges and gifts as usual. Ehrman's laconic style and soft sell is as gentle as his way of working with contractors and the architect. He wrote this identical letter to Frank Apt, James L. Fyfe, and others, on March 25: "The writer has been assigned the privilege of seeing you about a supplemental subscription towards making up the annual deficit, which amounts to about $500. I shall not have the time to call on all those on my list, so am writing you and two or three others in lieu of a personal call to explain that our operating expenses are somewhat greater than in the old church, etc, etc, etc, and closing with the usual appeal."

The Ladies Social Union had already donated over $800 to the building fund, so that traditional source of operating funds was out of the picture.[5] Additional funds were also needed for the final payments on the building and its furnishings, beyond the

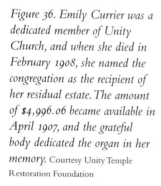

Figure 36. Emily Currier was a dedicated member of Unity Church, and when she died in February 1908, she named the congregation as the recipient of her residual estate. The amount of $4,996.06 became available in April 1907, and the grateful body dedicated the organ in her memory. Courtesy Unity Temple Restoration Foundation

amounts already pledged and the $6,500 in loans contracted in 1906 and 1907, and members of the parish were constantly reminded of the need to make good on their unredeemed financial pledges to the building fund. Fortunately, the completion of the probate of the will of Emily Currier (fig. 36), a congregant who had made the church the residual beneficiary of her estate and who had died in February of 1908, produced a final bequest of $4,996.06; that amount became available on April 17, 1909.[6] Knowing of the imminent arrival of the funds, the congregation resolved to use the money to pay for the organ and dedicated it to Emily Currier's memory.[7]

The congregation was shocked when, just two months after the annual meeting, Dr. Johonnot, the minister, submitted a letter of resignation to the board:

> Now even before the burning of our former place of worship, I had seriously considered whether my work in your

behalf was not practically finished. But the burning of our Church and the need of re-building seemed to me a plain call of duty to remain and do this new work. Yet it has been constantly in my mind that, with the completion of the new building, it might be best for both the society and for myself that my pastorate should come to an end. Now that the task of building is practically finished, I find the conclusion that I have done all that I can do for you become a conviction.[8]

Figure 37. The interior of Unity House is shown here, set up for services, while the Temple itself was nearing completion. Seating arrangements were less than ideal, as there was no clear view from the north and south portions of the space. In classic Wright fashion, he had a Winged Nike sculpture on one of the ledges.
Photo reprinted from *Cement World*, February 15, 1909

A committee of six members was appointed by President Roberts to help the trustees consider both the substance and the implications of the resignation. As a result of their deliberations, another meeting of the Society was called for June 11, at which time they voted on an informal ballot as to whether or not there was a desire for Dr. Johonnot to continue as pastor. The vote was 98 in favor of and 16 against asking him to remain, with an unrecorded number of abstentions. The body recessed, and a committee of two was sent to inform the minister of the results of the vote. When they returned, they brought a letter from Dr. Johonnot, thanking the congregants for their support and offering to reconsider. He did so, and countered with an offer of a resignation effective one year later, on July 1, 1910. The congregation then accepted the resignation with both thanks and regrets.[9]

Once again, as with the resignation of Dr. Johonnot's predecessor, Reverend Chapin, the minister was resigning while still enjoying widespread and substantial support within the congregation and with no immediate prospects for another pulpit. The wording of their resignation letters was startlingly similar, each noting that they thought their work had come to an end, that there was nothing more that they could do for the congregation. As Johonnot's letter made clear, he had already reached such a conclusion several years earlier and had only remained through the difficult construction period out of a sense of duty. And while it may be difficult for the lay person today to comprehend why these two pastors, both so important in the lives of their congregation, felt the need to sever their ties just when things were going well, it is certainly easy to understand how demanding the previous four years had been for Johonnot.

While there had been meaningful and interesting challenges, in regard to the design of the new building and the preparation of *The New Edifice* booklet, the four-year period from the fire through the completion of the building must have been more debilitating and frustrating than rewarding. There were endless special meetings to attend, the annoyance of running services and functioning without a proper office—in a rented space—for almost three years, and the frustrations at seeing the membership slip away in the years before the new building was completed. Seeing the crowds return for the first service in Unity House and then, a year later, for the first in the Temple itself, must have reinforced his most negative feelings about the depth of commitment of many of the congregants. His offer to stay for an additional year indicates both the level of his own commitment and his genuine appreciation of the fact that his flock wanted him to remain as their pastor, but it is also a reflection of his desire to start anew after the building was completed and in full operation. Being aware of political and economic realities as he was, he undoubtedly realized that it would be much easier to attract a new pastor with a newly completed building and the concomitant increase in attendance in place. In that regard, it is not unlike the phenomenon encountered today, when a museum director, university president, or library director retires or resigns after that completion of a major addition, a totally new building or a substantial overhaul of the administration, or the completion of a major fund-raising campaign.

Most of the remaining minor matters of decoration were completed in the late spring, and many (but not all) of the financial matters were finally resolved. The board's dispute with Foster & Glidden remained at an impasse, and matters became even worse with the dissolution of the partnership. Wilmot Glidden bought out his partners, Foster and Clifton, the latter being the partner who, as discussed above, was resident in Buffalo. The last letter written on the Foster & Glidden letterhead provides an appeal for funds, an explanation of the circumstances, and a legal threat, "As we are closing our books having sold our stock, tools, Machinery, etc to Wilmot Glidden & Son we have only a limited time to collect on all old accounts. A check mailed to Foster & Glidden at the old address will be duly credited to your account. After Sept 10 all old accounts will be in the hands of our attorney."[10] Although there

Figure 38. Looking at an early photo of Unity Temple from the north, we can see the imprint of the wooden forms that held the concrete as it was being poured. The lines indicate the level of each successive pour. Later refinishing has obscured this aspect of the construction process.

is no record of a successful resolution of the contractor's claim at that time, the matter must have been settled amicably. The issues that were not resolved before the dedication of the church certainly were to continue to appear in the records of ongoing disputes and in legal action in the years ahead.

As mentioned in the previous chapter, William Lees, the plumbing and heating contractor called in to rectify the heating problem was contacted by Ehrman to have the radiators in the Auditorium painted prior to the start of the new church year and the long postponed dedication of the new edifice. The building committee chairman's letter to Lees is quintessential Ehrman:

May I presume upon your kindness again? This time to ask the man that does your radiator painting to finish the radiators in Unity Church the early part of the coming week. They should be colored to match the wall spaces behind them, and I understand the cost for this work is regularly about $.02 per foot, and I estimate the number of feet from the data you gave me about 1750, which should bring the cost of doing the work to about $35.00. If the painter is able under the circumstances to shade this price somewhat, I am sure that such action will be very much appreciated.

The main thing, however, is the doing of the work not later than the middle of the week, as Unity Church is to be dedicated on the 26th, and we ought to have a few days in which to get rid of the paint odor.[11]

On Sunday, September 26, four years and almost four months after the old church was destroyed by fire, the new home of Unity Church was dedicated, with the pastor officiating. In order to recognize the structure and to honor the minister, the printed sheet *The Act of Dedication*, was imprinted with a picture of Dr. Johonnot superimposed over the corner of the illustration of the building (fig. 39). In addition to the various local and religious leaders and dignitaries in attendance were both Wright's uncle, the minister Jenkin Lloyd Jones, and the president of the American Unitarian Association, Samuel A. Eliot. The architect, according to his own account, did not attend:

This building, however, is finished and the Sunday for dedication arrives.

I do not want to go. Stay at home.

When the church was opened the phone began to ring. Happy contented voices are heard in congratulation. Finally weary, I take little Francie by the hand to go out into the air to get away from it all. Enough.

Figure 39. When the building was at long last dedicated on September 26, 1909, a handout gave the responsive readings that were a part of the service related to the dedication. In the upper-left corner is a photo of the new building, with an inset of the pastor, Dr. Johonnot.
Courtesy Unity Temple Restoration Foundation

But just as my hat goes on my head, another ring, a prosaic voice, Mr. Skillin's: "Take back all I said....Light everywhere—all pleased."

"Hear well?"

"Yes, see and hear fine—see it all now."

"I'm glad."

"Goodbye." At last the doubting member, sincere in praise, a good sport besides.

Francie got tossed in the air. She came down with a squeal of delight.[12]

It was Wright's great moment of triumph. Yet, by the date of the dedication, Mueller had overspent by almost $12,000, or over one-third of the original contract cost (the final bills are not all accounted for, and there are some contradictions among sources). He was soon to declare bankruptcy. Moreover, within the month,

Wright was to leave Oak Park, his practice, and his wife and children, when he left for Europe with the stated purpose of working with the German publisher Ernst Wasmuth on the proposed book of his designs, but accompanied by Mamah Cheney, his former client and neighbor—now his lover.

The members of the congregation, the dignitaries assembled for the dedication, and the local press were all enthusiastic about the completed building, and there were, indeed, kudos from all quarters. None of the written praise, however, matched the eloquence, directness, and prophetic recognition of the importance of the new building as well as the board of trustees' resolution of thanks that was adopted at the annual meeting following the dedication. It was those same trustees who, in spite of all the financial problems (some yet unresolved at that time), the incredible delays, and the problems inherent in both the materials and the innovative design, knew that they were the fortunate recipients of something very special. And the adoption of the following resolution goes far beyond the normal expressions of thanks and self-praise so common at the dedication of public buildings. It indicates a level of awareness unusual and critical recognition equally rare in the history of patronage:

> The members of the Unity Church Society, in annual meeting assembled, desire to place on record their appreciation of the new church edifice.
>
> The new building is a noble, dignified, beautiful and inspiring example of architecture and most admirably adapted to the various needs and activities of the church.
>
> Because of its uniqueness in style and construction it is set apart as a thing by itself, at once honoring and distinguishing both its designer and its possessors.
>
> Because of its simplicity, beauty and artistic effects it cannot but exert a refining and elevating influence upon all who frequent its portals.

We believe the new structure will grow in honor and favor both with the parish and the community.

We extend to the architect, Mr. Frank Lloyd Wright, our most hearty congratulations upon the wonderful achievement embodied in the new edifice and further extend to him our most sincere thanks for the great service which, through the building, he has rendered to the parish and to the community.

We believe the building will long endure as a monument to his artistic genius and that, so long as it endures, it will stand forth as a masterpiece in art and architecture.[13]

AFTERWORD

The building was completed and dedicated; there were only minor unmet issues to be resolved, and the congregation had already shown its appreciation and approval at the dedication. Even Mr. Skillin had weighed in with sincere praise. We have seen that, even before the building was completed, there had been positive response to it, both from the congregation and in the local press.

Now, a full century after that dedication, it seems that this is a most appropriate time to examine the reputation of the building after that euphoric first response, and in light of both its status as a National Historic Landmark (since 1971) and the thousands of people who visit from all over the world annually.

We have noted that the local newspaper of record commented on even the earliest known designs for the building, and additional articles and opinion pieces in *Oak Leaves* recorded the ongoing development of the building. Even after the opening service, a year before the heating problems forced the congregation to hold their services in Unity House, the press report was enthusiastic about the light, acoustics, and general appearance. That, in turn, caused both professionals and lay people to visit the building even before the completion and dedication. The widely read and highly respected *Inland Architect* had also referenced Wright's work and his stature during the construction and after its completion as well.

As I pointed out in the introduction, most scholars have admired the building without questioning Wright's account of its creation. In this book, we have examined that creation and creative process, and it is hoped that we now understand what happened here more fully. However, the details may enrich the experience, but not substitute for it. Perhaps that realization is why the hundreds of volumes on American and/or twentieth-century architecture that include the building have illustrated it and said little beyond a bare description of its appearance and construction technique.

Much has been made of and debated about the creation of an ecclesiastical structure made of concrete; tourists and scholars alike have noted the way one is led into the sanctuary through many turns and surprises, and the respect for the aesthetics, acoustics, and plan of the building is shared by all. Wright had already experimented with concrete, though not on a public structure like a church; he had already utilized the turns and twists before reaching the heart of a building in several homes within blocks of Unity Temple; his overall aesthetic and skill in decorative touches had already won him commissions throughout the Chicago area and beyond.

Yet Unity Temple remains more than the joining of those individual accomplishments, more than the sum of its parts. Understanding the theology behind Unitarianism is valuable for the worshipper, appreciating the acoustics when attending a concert in the sanctuary deepens our admiration for Wright's technical awareness, and admiring the way the architect incorporated various aspects of decoration from other cultures increases our respect for his skill in adapting and integrating forms. But the experience of Unity Temple is not about the isolation of any of those variables—it is about a total experience.

After the completion of Unity Temple, and after leaving Oak Park with Mamah Cheney, Wright was to have an extremely long, prolific, and distinguished career, in several parts. In the first few years were the completion of the projects under way in the Chicago area, the publication of his work in the noted Wasmuth Edition, the Midway Gardens, among other projects. Then there was the period of the creation of the first Taliesin in his home area of Spring Green, Wisconsin, the great Imperial Hotel in Japan, the start of his California career, and the introspective reexamination—and recreation of self—in the writing of his *Autobiography*. In the last period, there is the extremely fertile period of such master-pieces as Fallingwater, some of his great ecclesiastic architecture, and, finally, the Guggenheim Museum.

Reiterating Wright's own reaction to the building, as noted in the introduction, "When I finished Unity Temple, I had it. I knew I had the beginning of a great thing, a great truth in architecture," it is clear that the architect himself continued to respect and appre-ciate what he had accomplished, deepening his own valuation of the building rather than suffering from any second thoughts. Indeed, thinking back on the hundreds of buildings he had built and the many more that had never left the drawing board, and with all the critical, professional, and public acclaim he enjoyed, when asked which was his favorite building, Wright was to say with simple final-ity, "Unity Temple is my contribution to modern architecture."

The critics and architectural historians have all praised the building, with some giving more credit than others for the origi-nality of the design or the degree of innovation in the use of tech-niques and materials. The contemporary critic and biographer Ada Louise Huxtable, after noting various contributions and factors, succinctly pointed out both the value and importance of the build-ing, concluding, "It is something more—a humanistic concept that needs no conventional religious forms or symbols to express the ideal the congregation requested—the unity of God and man."[1]

The experience of the viewer, standing outside and looking at the building, but far more, sitting in the auditorium, validates and justifies both Huxtable's conclusion and Wright's own description of "a noble room," and each will likely concur with the master.

NOTES

Introduction

1. From a talk to the Taliesin Fellowship on August 13, 1952. Quoted in Pfeiffer and Nordland, *Frank Lloyd Wright: The Realm of Ideas*, 13.

2. Siry, *Unity Temple*, 227.

3. Ibid.

4. Wright, *A Testament*, 1957, and elsewhere.

Chapter 1: Unity Church to 1905

1. The citizens of the recently settled area were not immune from the kind of religious debates that were sweeping the country, and particularly the post–Civil War developments that grew out of the moves to institutionalize belief in both the Unitarian and the Universalist groups in their historic first conventions of 1865.

2. The "Great Chicago Fire" of October 1871 destroyed most of the official records and the documentation of the congregation's incorporation: as the group had not completed the construction of its first building, all records were apparently kept at the downtown business office of one of the members of the board of trustees, and the fire consumed whatever was in that office. Much of the material on the early years of the congregation is taken from Chulak, *A People Moving thru Time*.

3. Gale had moved to Chicago as a child, when his Universalist father, Abram, became one of the pioneer settlers of the new city. Both Gales speculated in land in suburban Chicago (Galewood) and both moved to the fledgling town of Oak Ridge—later Oak Park—in 1863. According to one of the oldest inhabitants of the village, by 1867 the Gales were wealthy enough to build one of the very few brick houses in the community, a visible sign of their high status. See Cook, *Little Old Oak Park, 1837–1902*, chapter 1.

4. There were several mergers and changes in affiliation over the years until the humanist inspired Statement of Faith adopted by the Universalists at their 1935 convention removed the objections of

the other members and caused the parish to officially affiliate with the Universalist denomination that same year. With the merger of the American Unitarian Association and the Universalist Church of America in 1961, the congregation became the Unity Temple Unitarian Universalist Congregation in Oak Park. For a discussion of the slow but inexorable move toward union of the two groups, see David Robinson, *The Unitarians and the Universalists.*

5. I am indebted to Glory Southwind of Chicago for sharing her ongoing research on Chapin with me and pointing out the several areas of the minister's activities and friendships during her years in Oak Park.

6. See the membership, baptismal, and contribution records belonging to the church and still in its possession. Throughout this volume, material in the archives of the congregation will be designated with the following abbreviations: those documents kept in the building will be referenced as UUCOP-UT; those documents deposited at the Oak Park Public Library will be referenced as UUCOP-OPL.

7. The references to the need for a new building are never explained in the literature.

8. A copy of the solicitation letter is in the archives, UUCOP-UT, in the appropriate annual envelope.

9. From the record of minutes of annual and special meetings of the Unity Church parish. Unless otherwise noted, all quotes and information attributed to the minutes of either the parish meetings or those of the board of trustees refer to those records in the archives of the congregation now known as the Unity Temple Unitarian Universalist Congregation in Oak Park. All original spellings and punctuation are maintained; the use of capitals is, as well, when the handwriting can be deciphered to the point of certainty. When there is doubt as to whether a capital or small letter was intended, contemporary usage will prevail.

10. Requesting a recommendation on such an important issue in a month's time might suggest that the answer was already known, and that might be the case. However, when we remember how quickly the original founders of the church moved to organize and examine

the timelines for other major decisions, it seems that the request for a report before the summer vacation was hardly out of line.

11. Chulak, *A People Moving thru Time*, 19.
12. *Oak Leaves* (Oak Park, Illinois), June 10, 1905, 12–13.
13. The letter sent to Reverend Johonnot by the secretary to the board of trustees of the First Baptist Church of Oak Park has been preserved and documents the generosity of one church toward another: "Resolved: That we express to the Pastor and Members of the Unity Church, our regrets and sincere sympathies at the loss of their Church Building by fire, and, that we offer to them the use of our building for any or all of their services until such time as other arrangements have been made."
14. UUCOP-OPL.
15. *Oak Leaves*, June 10, 1909, 1.
16. The complete makeup of the committees is as follows: Ways and Means: H.A. Taylor, W.S. Holden, C.A. Sharpe, D.C. Tunch, Chas. Woodard; Site: J.H. Heald, E.R. Haase, C.S. Hafner; Plans: R.F. Johonnot, Mrs. A.W. Bryant, E.H. Ehrman, Dwight Jackson, Mrs. John Lewis; Building: C.E. Roberts, Frank Adams, H.P. Harnd.
17. Minutes of the Ladies Social Union, June 29, 1905, UUCOP-UT.
18. Letter from Emmons Howard to Reverend R.F. Johonnot, dated June 21, 1905, UUCOP-OPL.
19. The site committee was asked to report their findings directly to the president and board of trustees, though no deadline was given.
20. *Oak Leaves*, August 12, 1905, 1.
21. Ibid.
22. Ibid.

Chapter 2: The Architect and His Plans

1. Minutes of the special meeting of the board of trustees, August 30, 1905, UUCOP-UT.
2. Ibid.
3. Siry's article, "Frank Lloyd Wright's Unity Temple and Architecture for Liberal Religion in Chicago, 1885–1909," is the first scholarly investigation of aspects of the sources and circumstances behind the design of the building.

4. Wright himself comments on the relationship with Rev. Chapin in his autobiographical volume, and authors such as Grant C. Manson have incorrectly translated that personal association to membership. Manson, in discussing the award of the commission to Wright states, "Although the Wrights had been members of the congregation for many years, it was an unexpected move." Manson, *Frank Lloyd Wright to 1910: The First Golden Age*, 158.

5. From All Souls Church annual reports found at the Regenstein Library, University of Chicago.

6. See his listing in the parish directory for the 1904–1905 membership year, UUCOP-UT.

7. Various members of the Wright family had relationships with the Unitarian congregation, a son in a youth group for a year, and Anna Wright, the architect's mother, belonged to a woman's auxiliary, but Frank and Catherine are absent from the annual lists of members, donors, etc.

8. Thanks to Ronald Moline for his information and calling my attention to these archived materials. See his undated two-page piece, "From the Archives," 2006.

9. Ibid.

10. From a flyer dated August 28, 1905, and mailed to all members of the Parish. UUCOP-UT.

11. Minutes of the board of trustees, September 3, 1905, UUCOP-UT.

12. Wright, *An Autobiography* (New York: Horizon Press, 1977), 177. This edition, with the text reproducing that of the 1943 edition and adding the previously omitted sixth section, "Broadacre City," is the most widely available and, unless otherwise noted, will be the source of all quotes cited from *An Autobiography*.

13. Ibid.

14. Ibid., 178.

15. Ibid.

16. Ibid.

17. Ibid., 177.

18. Ibid., 183.

19. Ibid., 183.

20. Ibid.

21. There is no mention of how the four candidates were narrowed down to one, nor do the minutes of the board of trustees mention the matter of an architect and plans, from September 3 until this meeting of December 17, from which the information has been derived.

22. Minutes of the meeting of the board of trustees, January 2, 1906, UUCOP-UT.

23. Minutes of an adjourned special meeting of the board of trustees, January 4, 1906, UUCOP-UT.

24. Minutes of the meeting of board of trustees, January 14, 1906, UUCOP-UT.

25. Wright, *An Autobiography*, 183.

26. Minutes of the meeting of board of trustees, January 14, 1906, UUCOP-UT.

27. Minutes of an adjourned meeting of board of trustees, January 21, 1906, UUCOP-UT.

28. Changing nomenclature is not limited to the ways and means committee; the minutes of the meetings of the board of directors refer to the chief executive officer as the president of the board, but his title appears in several places, including the brochure on the building, as the chairman of the board of trustees. There never seems to be any doubt as to the identity of the person being discussed, but when committees combine or recombine, there might be confusion as to the exact committee being chaired by the individual being named as chairman.

29. Minutes of an adjourned meeting of the board of trustees, held on January 21, 1906, UUCOP-UT.

30. Ibid.

31. Minutes of an adjourned meeting of the board of trustees, February 7, 1906, UUCOP-UT. In *An Autobiography*, Wright was to tell us that the available church funds amounted to $45,000, and that they only went a little over budget.

32. Ibid.

33. From a letter dated March 4, 1906, written to White's friend, Walter Willcox, in Brooks, *Writings on Wright*, 90. Charles E. White Jr.

(1876–1936) worked in Wright's office, as a draftsman, from early in 1904 until he left to set up his own local practice a few weeks before this letter was written.

34. Ibid. This statement is valuable for its corroboration of two different matters, the date of drawings themselves, and that the price of the building was known to be well under the $45,000 cited in *An Autobiography*, even by Wright's junior staff members.

35. *Oak Leaves*, Saturday, February 24, 1906, 1. The story is accompanied by what must be the first appearance of the often-illustrated drawing of the west façade of Unity Temple by Marion Mahony.

36. Minutes of a meeting of the board of trustees, March 4, 1906, UUCOP-UT. The motion contained the curious provision that the booklet being mandated by the board be published with no expense to the Church Society, and there is no indication as to how the publication was to be funded.

Chapter 3: Unity Temple: Design and Justification

1. Wright, *An Autobiography*, 178.
2. Ibid.
3. Ibid., 179.
4. *Oak Leaves*, February 24, 1906, 3.
5. Ibid., 3, 5.
6. Wright, *An Autobiography*, 183.
7. The notice of the awarding of the commission to Wright was announced in *Construction News* 20 (September, 23, 1905), 235, and mentioned that the architect had drawn plans of a building to be constructed of brick and stone.
8. *An Autobiography*, 178.
9. Minutes of the meeting of the board of trustees held on April 28, 1906.
10. The brochure consisted of fifteen pages of text and plans, lists the members of the boards of trustees for 1905 and 1906 and the members of the various building-related committees, and was published by the Chicago printing firm of Marshall-Jackson Co., a company owned by a member of the congregation. It has been reprinted several times in recent years (without imprint

information) and is currently still available for purchase. There seem to be no other references to the New Unity Church Club, and we can only assume that it was an ad hoc organization formed in response to the board mandate for a brochure that would not be printed at the expense of the congregation. The brochure committee lists Charles S. Woodard, R.F. Johonnot, and Frank Lloyd Wright as the members.

11. Brendan Gill, *Many Masks*, 175.

12. The brochure pages are unnumbered, and this statement marks the beginning of the text.

13. From a letter of George Elmslie to Frank Lloyd Wright, October 30, 1932, Northwest Architectural Archive, University of Minnesota.

14. Unfortunately, the surviving church records provide no clear indication of the division of the congregation—or parish—between the Universalists and the Unitarians; church, rather than parish, membership is not itself an accurate gauge. First of all, by the turn of the century, some of the newer members had affiliated with Unity Church with little or no awareness of either its historical origins and divisions, nor did they necessarily have any connection to either the Unitarians or the Universalists. They simply accepted the reality of a liberal church. According to veteran members of the church, a second and even overlapping reason is that some members, even Universalists by choice (and we have no idea how many), were insufficiently interested in the problem of affiliation to opt for membership in the church within the parish.

15. David Robinson, *The Unitarians and the Universalists*, 285.

16. For a full discussion of the range of the activities and impact of Jenkin Lloyd Jones, see Lyttle, *Freedom Moves West*.

17. Tucker, *Prophetic Sisterhood*, 106.

18. Lyttle, *Freedom Moves West*, 158.

19. Tucker, *Prophetic Sisterhood*, 107.

Chapter 4: Building Unity Temple, Part I

1. The club had been founded on January 23, 1906, with the enthusiastic support of the minister. Several undated membership lists of

the organization remain in the files of the church, two listing Mr. and Mrs. Frank Lloyd Wright and one with their names crossed out.

2. H. Eilenberger, a Chicago-based general contractor, had first submitted a bid for $51,459 on April 21, with the following proposal: "We beg to also submit another scheme of construction that we have figured out whereby we can eliminate a tent and at the same time do the work so that we can save a considerable amount off this bid. If our proposition is such that you can consider a revised scheme, we will be pleased to submit the matter to you."

3. Wright, *An Autobiography*, 183.

4. Minutes of the board of trustees, April 28, 1906.

5. Ibid.

6. Minutes of an adjourned special meeting of the board of trustees, April 30, 1906.

7. Minutes of the meeting of board of trustees, May 6, 1906.

8. In the letter from Charles White to Walter Willcox, quoted above, White says: "Walter Griffin has resigned, and will practice in Chicago. His place is taken by Wright's brother-in-law, who comes from a position in Armor's [*sic*] Beef concern. A good businessman (no experience in architecture) and a fine fellow. Suppose he will eventually write specifications and superintending."

9. Minutes of a meeting of the board of trustees, May 20, 1906.

10. Specifications, p. 8. The thirty-eight pages of specifications are in the special local author collection of the Oak Park Library, on extended loan from UUCOP.

11. In a letter to President Adams, dated June 12, Mueller indicated the length of his absence by stating, "In reference to your communications to filing application for the bond with the Metropolitan Surety Co, wish to say that this matter has been overlooked on account of my being out of town and I have today filled out the application."

12. Letter from Wright addressed to "The Trustees of Unity Church," dated July 10, 1906, UUCOP-OPL.

13. The "experiments" consisted of twenty panels comprised of the different sizes and types of gravel used to create various concrete finishes. Each was two feet, six inches square.

14. Letter from E.H. Ehrman to William Adams, dated July 13, 1906. UUCOP-OPL.

15. The requests for payment were all submitted by Paul Mueller on March 29, 1909, and almost all were rejected as being either unauthorized or done at the option of the contractor.

16. Minutes of a special meeting of the board of trustees held on September 30, 1906.

17. Letter from E.H. Ehrman to Paul F.P. Mueller, dated January 30, 1907, UUCOP-OPL.

18. Ibid.

19. Ibid.

20. Minutes of the board of trustees meeting of November 4, 1906.

21. Minutes of the February 3 meeting of the board of trustees.

22. Letter from Ehrman to Mueller, February 23, 1907, UUCOP-OPL.

23. Ehrman to Wright, March 14, 1907, UUCOP-UT.

24. Wright to Ehrman, undated, UUCOP-UT. A handwritten date of 3/18/07 appears on the original letter.

25. Unity Church: Annual Parish Meeting—1907, UUCOP-UT.

26. Minutes of the 37th Annual Meeting of the Unity Church Society, March 25, 1907, UUCOP-UT.

27. Minutes of the Annual Meeting of the Ladies Social Union, January 30, 1907, UUCOP-UT.

28. Ibid.

29. Ibid.

30. *Oak Leaves*, March 30, 1907, 1.

31. Minutes of the board of trustees meeting of April 7, 1907, UUCOP-UT.

32. Treasurer's report contained in the minutes of the board of trustees meeting of June 2, 1907, UUCOP-UT.

33. Letter from Ehrman to Wright, June 11, 1907, UUCOP-OPL.

34. Minutes of the August 28, 1907, meeting of the board of trustees, UUCOP-UT.

35. Letter from Mueller to building committee, Unity Church, dated September 13, 1907, UUCOP-OPL.

36. Rodney F. Johonnot to "Dear Friends of Unity Church," September 4, 1907, UUCOP-UT.

Chapter 5: Building Unity Temple, Part II

1. *Oak Leaves*, September 21, 1907.
2. Ibid. The color of the interior had changed several times after mid-century, and only the most recent scientific color analysis has produced a color combination that conforms to this written description.
3. Minutes of the meeting of the Ladies Social Union, September 20, 1907, UUCOP-UT.
4. Letter from Ehrman to Wright, September 24, 1907, UUCOP-UT. In Drummond's letter of September 18, he had pointed out that he had delayed paying Bauer as long as possible, considering that Wright was out of town and had not signed a certificate, but that "as the man is in great need and he has been patient I cannot ask him to wait until Mr. Wright's return." UUCOP-UT.
5. Letter from Foster & Glidden Co. of Oak Park to E.H. Ehrman, November 4, 1907, and Ehrman to F&G, November 7, 1907, UUCOP-OPL.
7. Minutes of a special meeting of the board of trustees, November 11, 1907, UUCOP-UT.
8. Letter from Adams to Mueller, November 16, 1907, UUCOP-OPL.
9. Letter from Adams to Mueller, November 20, 1907, UUCOP-OPL.
10. Letter from Ehrman to Bryant Brothers of Forest Park, March 3, 1908, and following, UUCOP-OPL.
11. Letter from Foster & Glidden to Wright, January 7, 1908, UUCOP-OPL.
12. Ehrman to Wright in March 19 and Wright to board of trustees on March 20, 1908, UUCOP-OPL.
13. Minutes of the 38th annual meeting of the Unity Church Society, March 30, 1908, UUCOP-UT.
15. Adams to Mueller and Ehrman to Mueller, both April 7, 1908, UUCOP-OPL.
17. Letter from Samuel W. Packard to E.H. Ehrman, June 2, 1908, UUCOP-OPL.
18. E.O. Gale to E.H. Ehrman, June 1, 1908, UUCOP -OPL.

20. Minutes of the board of trustees meeting of July 5, 1908.
21. Letters from Adams to Mueller and Adams to Roberts, both dated July 7, 1908, UUCOP-OPL.
22. Letter from Foster & Glidden to E.H. Ehrman, August 7, 1908, UUCOP-OPL. The many projects shared by Wright, Mueller, and Foster & Glidden included the Larkin Building in Buffalo, Unity Temple, and at least several homes in Oak Park. Mueller also contracted the E-Z Polish Building and, later, Midway Gardens and the Imperial Hotel in Japan. It has not been determined whether Foster & Glidden participated in any of these other projects.
23. An open letter to all subscribers to the building fund, sent on September 10, 1908, and signed by both President William G. Adams and James H. Heald Jr., the treasurer, UUCOP-UT.

Chapter 6: Completing Unity Temple

1. Letter from the plans committee to the board of trustees, March 14, 1908, UUCOP-OPL.
2. Unsigned letter from President Adams to Paul F. P. Mueller, March 30, 1908, UUCOP-OPL. A letter to Wright, written on May 20, references his submission of the report to Mueller and establishes his authorship.
3. Letter from American Seating Company to W.G. Adams, September 21, 1908, UUCOP-OPL.
4. Letter form E.H. Ehrman to American Seating Company, of Chicago, September 16, 1908, in the archive of UUCOP-OPL.
5. Gill, *Many Masks*, 189.
6. Letter from Joseph J. Vogel to William G. Adams, October 12, 1908, UUCOP-OPL.
7. Letter from Emmons Howard to Rev. R.F. Johonnot, June 21, 1905, UUCOP-OPL. The Howard firm was located in Westfield, Massachusetts. Other firms that contacted the church were headquartered in Hartford, Connecticut; Erie, Pennsylvania; Brattleboro, Vermont; and Hagerstown, Maryland; four of the firms were Chicago-based.
8. The firm of Hillgreen, Lane, & Co. went further in their solicitation than the others, stating that they had recently completed an

organ for the Paulist Fathers in Chicago and suggesting that it might well be of the size needed by Unity Church; and in a fit of praise, they informed the minister that the organist, a Father Finn "is one of the best musicians in the city, and he will take pleasure in displaying the organ to you, and explaining its appointments. Do not hesitate in calling for the privilege of hearing the instrument." Letter to Pastor, Unity Church, October 28, 1907, in the UUCOP-OPL.

9. Letter from Edwin Ehrman to Frank Lloyd Wright, May 22, 1907, UUCOP-OPL.

10. Letter from Lyon & Healy to Edwin Ehrman, July 19, 1907, UUCOP-OPL.

11. Letter from Edwin Ehrman to LaMotte Wells of Lyon & Healy, July 26, 1907, UUCOP-OPL.

12. Letter from Edwin Ehrman to Frank Lloyd Wright, October 2, 1907, UUCOP-OPL.

13. In a letter to Charles F. Rowe, the consultant hired to help the congregation get the correct organ for the space, Ehrman wrote: "I would say, that personally I do not believe it wise to crowd the matter of the organ space allotted by the architect at this time, as it might serve to complicate rather than to straighten out the matter." Ehrman to Charles F. Rowe, of Chicago, December 2, 1907, UUCOP-UT.

14. Letter from Edwin Ehrman to Estey Organ Company of Brattleboro, Vermont, September 13, 1907, UUCOP-OPL. Most of the organ companies agreed; they just didn't see how they could proceed. W. Kimball Co., one of the Chicago firms to contact the church informed Ehrman that "the truth is that the plans were of such a peculiar character that it is almost impossible to make any results that are satisfactory, out of them." They also noted that they had waited until the building was actually closer to completion so they could see the actual space in person. Letter from A.D. Longmore to E.H. Ehrman, September 7, 1907, UUCOP-OPL.

15. Letters from Hillgreen, Lane, & Co, to Rev. R.F. Johonnot and E.H. Ehrman, November 14 and 16, 1907, UUCOP-OPL. The correspondence between Rowe and the various organ-building

firms has not been located, and our knowledge of their interaction is only known through copies of Ehrman's letters to him and through reference and inference in the extant correspondence between the building committee and the companies themselves.

16. Letter from Ehrman to Rowe, December 2, 1907, UUCOP-UT.

17. Letter from M.P. Moeller of Hagerstown, Maryland, to E.H. Erman [*sic*], November 11, 1907, UUCOP-OPL. The fragmentary correspondence with the various firms is sufficient to trace the progress on the project with clarity.

18. Letter from Isabel Roberts to Ehrman, March 20, 1908, UUCOP-OPL. It is interesting to note that, when serious negotiations about the space took place, this firm recommended a smaller organ than they had at first, and that they failed to surface as a finalist when the decision was finally made.

19. The seven firms, in descending order of their ratings were: Kimball, Lyon & Healy; Estey; Felgemaker (Erie); Moller, Hillgreen Lane; and J.W. Steere.

20. W.S. Coburn to Mr. Hemington, August 29, 1908, UUCOP-UT. Francis Hemington's affiliation with the church is not made clear through the extant references to him, but later correspondence indicates that he either lived or worked at 421 North Boulevard in Oak Park.

21. E.H. Ehrman to Hook-Eastings Co., on October 26, 1908, UUCOP-OPL. Essentially the same letter was sent to all those who had lately written and those who were to contact Ehrman at a later date.

22. The contract called for a completion date on or before December 23, 1908. It was signed by the two partners in the organ firm and by William Adams, president of the board of trustees of Unity Church.

23. E.H. Ehrman to Dr. Francis Hemington, April 13, 1912, UUCOP-OPL.

24. William G. Adams to H. Gensch of Chicago, October 20, 1908, UUCOP-OPL.

25. Brendan Gil has commented (*Many Masks*, 161) on Wright's "urnomania" and its impact on the group of Prairie School architects.

26. UUCOP-OPL contains an unsigned memo, dated October 21, 1908. Its references to a conversation with Wright, as well as to calls to both Ehrman and Roberts, convincingly argue for Adams as the writer.

27. W. Adams to H. Gensch, October 23, 1908, UUCOP-OPL.

28. Ibid.

29. As stated in the contract between Foster & Glidden Co. and Unity Church, dated September 24, 1906, UUCOP-UT.

30. Oral tradition has it that so much heat came through the walls during the first winter that the trees on Lake Street never lost their leaves.

31. Edwin H. Ehrman to Foster & Glidden Co., November 28, 1908, UUCOP-OPL. The writer expresses his concern at seeing no evidence of materials that would suggest that work was being done.

32. W.W. Glidden to E.H. Ehrman, November 30, 1908, UUCOP-OPL. I have reproduced the writer's unusual (Germanic?) usage, though ignoring his equally unusual division of paragraphs and the way he totally ignored the use of periods at the end of sentences.

33. E.H. Ehrman to Foster & Glidden, UUCOP-OPL. Ehrman also reminds the contractor that the two sides discussing possible modifications and the church making suggestions in no way diminishes the responsibility of the contractor to obtain approval for any changes or for the successful performance of the modified system.

34. That there is no surviving correspondence between the church and the contractor between the end of November and the middle of January (when Foster & Glidden's offer is referenced in a letter to Wright), in an otherwise detailed exchange of letters, leads one to the conclusion that there was a great deal of on-site and telephone contact about this matter. Given the nature of the problem, site visits by the contractor would certainly have been necessary.

35. William G. Adams to Frank Lloyd Wright, January 18, 1909, UUCOP-OPL. Adams also informed Wright that they would decide if the heating system was adequate after the new boiler was installed.

36. William G. Adams to Frank Lloyd Wright, January 19, 1909, UUCOP-OPL.
37. Frank Lloyd Wright to Foster & Glidden Co., January 20, 1909, UUCOP-OPL.
38. W.W. Glidden to Frank Lloyd Wright, January 21, 1909, UUCOP-OPL.
39. William G. Adams to Foster & Glidden Company, January 23, 1909, UUCOP-OPL.
40. W.W. Glidden to William G. Adams, January 25, 1909, UUCOP-OPL.
41. E.H. Ehrman to Foster & Glidden, January 30, 1909, UUCOP-OPL. These formal communications were usually typed on the stationery of Ehrman's firm, and with his initials followed by those of another, indicating the work of a staff secretary. But because this particular letter was written on a Saturday, it was written on notepaper, either at Ehrman's home or at the church.
42. The UUCOP-UT archives include Ehrman's handwritten record of the steam pressure and the temperature readings turned over by Mr. Hammond. The second sheet also includes the names, addresses, and telephone numbers of the other members of the building committee, clearly available in case of another emergency.
43. William Lees to E.H. Ehrman, March 10, 1909, UUCOP-OPL.
44. Ibid.
45. E.H. Ehrman to William Lees, March 11, 1909, UUCOP-OPL.
46. E.H. Ehrman to William Lees, September 18, 1909, UUCOP-OPL.

Chapter 7: Disaster to Dedication

1. Letter from Wright to William G. Adams, March 8, 1909.
2. Ibid.
3. Adams to Wright, March 12, 1909, UUCOP-UT.
4. Wright continues to make the case for money owed to Mueller, both for "extras" and for projects he felt were the legitimate responsibility of the church. Though the architect must have been getting Mueller's figures from the man himself (and probably in writing), there is no known record of such correspondence.

5. The L.S.U. had always been a major source of support for the congregation, but they had taken on such a large commitment ($2,331) toward the erection of the new building that they could not also contribute toward the operating expenses of the church.
6. Currier's will was filed in Probate Court of Cook County on March 25, 1908.
7. Minutes of the Annual Meeting of Unity Church, March 29, 1909, UUCOP-UT.
8. Minutes of a special meeting of the Society, May 30, 1909, UUCOP-UT.
9. Minutes of special meetings of June 11 and June 24, UUCOP-UT.
10. A.E. Clifton, treasurer, to an unspecified recipient (probably Ehrman), August 21, 1909, UUCOP-OPL.
11. E.H. Ehrman to Wm. Lees, September 18, 1909, UUCOP-OPL.
12. Wright, *An Autobiography*, 176. As the congregation had begun to worship in the Temple itself almost a year earlier, it is entirely possible—even probable—that Wright was conflating the events of the first services in the Auditorium with the official dedication. While some calls might well have come at the latter, it is less likely that regular church-going members of the congregation, like Skillin, would have failed to experience the acoustics and lighting of the building before the day of the dedication.
13. Minutes of the Annual Meeting of the Parish, March 1910, UUCOP-UT.

Afterword

1. Huxtable, *Frank Lloyd Wright: A Life*, 102.

BIBLIOGRAPHY

The following is a basic bibliography of sources and important books and articles that address the importance of Unity Temple and its place in Wright's architecture.

Archival Sources

Frank Lloyd Wright Archives, The Frank Lloyd Wright Foundation, Taliesin, Scottsdale, Arizona.

Northwest Architectural Archive, University of Minnesota.

Unity Temple Unitarian Universalist Congregation in Oak Park's Historical Files, Oak Park, Illinois.

Unity Temple Collection, Oak Park Public Library, Oak Park, Illinois.

Newspapers

Construction News

Oak Leaves, Archived at the Oak Park Public Library and the Historical Society of Oak Park and River Forest.

Published Sources

Berlage, H.P. *The Architectural Forum* (January 1938), 35.

Brooks, H. Allen, ed. *Writings on Wright: Selected Comment on Frank Lloyd Wright*. Cambridge, MA: MIT Press, 1981.

Cannon, Patrick F. *Hometown Architect: The Complete Buildings of Frank Lloyd Wright in Oak Park and River Forest, Illinois*. San Francisco: Pomegranate, 2006.

Chulak, Thomas A. *A People Moving thru Time: The History of the Unitarian Universalist Church in Oak Park*. Oak Park, IL: Unitarian Universalist Church in Oak Park, 1979.

Cook, May Estelle. *Little Old Oak Park, 1837–1902*. Oak Park, IL: privately printed, 1961.

Drexler, Arthur. *Drawings of Frank Lloyd Wright*. New York: Bramhall House, 1962.

Frank, Marie. "Theory of Pure Design and American Architectural Education in the Early 20th Century." *JSAH* 67, no. 2 (June 2008), 248–73.

Gannett, William C. *The House Beautiful*. River Forest, IL: Auvergne Press, 1896.

Gill, Brendan. *Many Masks: A Life of Frank Lloyd Wright*. New York: G.P. Putnam's Sons, 1987.

Graf, Otto Antonia. *Die Kunst des Quadrats: Zum Werk von Frank Lloyd Wright*. Vienna: H. Bohlau, 1983.

Gutheim, Frederick, ed. *Frank Lloyd Wright on Architecture: Selected Writings, 1894–1940*. New York: Duell, Sloan, and Pearce, 1941.

Hitchcock, Henry Russell. *In the Nature of Materials: The Buildings of Frank Lloyd Wright, 1887–1941*. New York: Duell, Sloan, and Pearce, 1942.

Holzhueter, John O. "Cudworth Beye, Frank Lloyd Wright, and the Yahara River Boathouse, 1905." *Wisconsin Magazine of History* 72, no. 3 (spring 1989), 163–98.

Horan, Nancy. *Loving Frank: A Novel*. New York: Ballantine Books, 2007.

Hugo, Victor. *Notre Dame de Paris*. Trans. Jessie Haynes. New York: New American Library, 1953.

Hunderman, Harry J. and Deborah Slaton, eds. *Unity Temple: Historic Structures Report*. Chicago: Wiss, Janney, Elstner Associates. 1987.

Huxtable, Ada Louise. *Frank Lloyd Wright: A Life*. New York: Penguin Books, 2004.

Isozaki, Arata. *MA. Space-Time in Japan*. New York: Cooper-Hewitt Museum, 2001. Catalogue of an exhibition.

Johonnot, Rodney F., ed. *The New Edifice of Unity Church*. Oak Park, IL: Unitarian Universalist Church in Oak Park, 1906.

Kaufmann, Edgar Jr. and Ben Raeburn, eds. *Frank Lloyd Wright: Writings and Buildings*. New York: New American Library, 1960.

Levine, Neil. *The Architecture of Frank Lloyd Wright*. Princeton, NJ: Princeton University Press, 1996.

Lyttle, Charles H. *Freedom Moves West: A History of the Western Unitarian Conference, 1852–1952*. Boston: Beacon Press, 1952.

Manson, Grant Carpenter. *Frank Lloyd Wright to 1910: The First Golden Age*. New York: Van Nostrand Reinhold, 1958.

McCarter, Robert. *Unity Temple: Frank Lloyd Wright*. London: Phaidon, 1997.

Nute, Kevin. *Frank Lloyd Wright and Japan: The Role of Traditional Japanese Art and Architecture in the Work of Frank Lloyd Wright*. New York: Van Nostrand Reinhold, 1993.

Pfeiffer, Bruce Brooks. *Frank Lloyd Wright Drawings*. New York: Harry N. Abrams, 1990.

———. *Frank Lloyd Wright Preliminary Studies, 1889–1916*. Edited by Yukio Futagawa. Tokyo: A.D.A. Edita, 1985.

Pfeiffer, Bruce Brooks and Gerald Nordland. *Frank Lloyd Wright: The Realm of Ideas*. Carbondale, IL: Southern Illinois University Press, 1988.

Robinson, David. *The Unitarians and the Universalists*. Westport, CT: Greenwood Press, 1985.

Scully, Vincent J. *Frank Lloyd Wright*. New York: George Braziller, 1960.

———. *Modern Architecture*. New York: George Braziller, 1961.

Siry, Joseph M. "Frank Lloyd Wright's Unity Temple and Architecture for Liberal Religion in Chicago, 1885–1909," *Art Bulletin* 73, no. 2 (June 1991), 257–82.

———. *Unity Temple: Frank Lloyd Wright and Architecture for Liberal Religion*. Cambridge: Cambridge University Press, 1996.

Tucker, Cynthia Grant. *Prophetic Sisterhood: Liberal Women Ministers of the Frontier, 1880–1930*. Boston: Beacon Press, 1990.

Twombly, Robert C. *Frank Lloyd Wright: His Life and Architecture*. New York: John Wiley and Sons, 1979.

van de Ven, Cornelis. *Space in Architecture*. Amsterdam: Van Grocum Assen, 1978.

Wright, Frank Lloyd. *Ausgefuhrte und Entwurfe von Frank Lloyd Wright*. Berlin: Ernst Wasmuth, 1910.

———. *An Autobiography*. New York: Longmans, Green, 1932.

———. *An Autobiography*. New York: Duell, Sloan, and Pearce, 1943.

———. *An Autobiography*. New York: Horizon Press, 1977.

———. *Collected Writings*. Edited by Bruce Brooks Pfeiffer. Vol. 1, *1894–1930*. New York: Rizzoli, 1992.

———. *The Future of Architecture*. New York: Horizon Press, 1953.

———. *A Testament*. New York: Bramhall, 1957.

ABOUT THE AUTHOR

DAVID M. SOKOL has had a 40-year career as a professor of art history and has taught at the University of Illinois at Chicago since 1971. He chaired the department of art history for 17 years, becoming professor emeritus in 2002.

In addition to teaching and writing on American and European art and architecture, Sokol has published articles and reviews on Frank Lloyd Wright and Unity Temple. He is the author of *Oak Park, Illinois: Continuity and Change.*

He served on the board of directors for the Unity Temple Restoration Foundation and the Frank Lloyd Wright Home and Studio Foundation, and currently serves on the Illinois Historic Sites Advisory Council.

Sokol lives in Oak Park, Illinois.